EXPLORING SCIENCE

SPACE

AN AMAZING FACT FILE AND HANDS-ON PROJECT BOOK

With 19 easy-to-do experiments and 300 exciting pictures

IAN GRAHAM • CONSULTANT: Dr GERAINT H JONES

ARMADILLO

This edition is published by Armadillo, an imprint of Anness Publishing Ltd,
108 Great Russell Street, London WC1B 3NA; info@anness.com

www.annesspublishing.com

If you like the images in this book and would like to
investigate using them for publishing, promotions or
advertising, please visit our website
www.practicalpictures.com for more information.

Publisher: Joanna Lorenz
Senior Editor: Neil Kelly
Photographer: John Freeman
Stylist: Melanie Williams
Designer: Caroline Grimshaw
Picture Researcher: Kay Rowley
Illustrator: Peter Bull Art Studio
Production Controller: Pirong Wang

The publishers would like to thank the following children, and their parents, for appearing
in this book: Mohammed Afsar, Harriet Bartholomew, James Capuyan, Joanne Fleck,
Mary Fleck, Otis Harrington, Stella-Rae James, Tommy Swaine-Jameson, Charlie Ray,
Jackie Ritah.

Manufacturer: Anness Publishing Ltd,
108 Great Russell Street, London WC1B 3NA, England
For Product Tracking go to:
www.annesspublishing.com/tracking
Batch: 7154-22958-1127

PICTURE CREDITS
b=bottom, t=top, c=central, l=left, r=right, SPL=Science Photo Library
Anglo-Australian Telescope Board/Image Select page 8tr; Chris Beetles, London,
UK/Bridgeman Art Library page 4cr; Daily Telegraph Colour Library page 44cr; © 1982
Don Dixon/TRH Pictures/NASM/NASA page 9bl; ESA page 57tl; ESO Information and
Photographic Service page 24bl; Genesis Space Photo Library pages 33cr, 33tl, 35tl, 37tl,
40cl, 41b, 56cl, 57cl; NASA pages 2t, 2br, 3br, 5br, 21tl, 21br, 24br, 34br, 37br, 42cl, 42cr,
42bl, 42br, 43tl, 43tr, 47c, 49br, 61bl, 62c, 63tl, 63cr, 63bl, 63br, 64br; NASA/JPL-
Caltec/MSSS page 53tr; NASA/Genesis Space Photo Library page 44tl; NASA/Science and
Society Photo Library pages 40cr, 48b; NASA/Space Charts pages 1, 36tr, 36br, 45tl, 57br;
NASA/SPL pages 4br, 8br, 19br, 32cl, 32bl, 35br, 40tr, 41tr, 44br, 45bl, 46tl, 52tl; Novosti
Photo Library pages 28cl, 28bl; Planet Earth Pictures pages 22tl, 25tl, 35bl, 37tr, 37cl, 49tl,
52bl, 53cl, 53bl; Science Museum/Science and Society Picture Library pages 2cl, 34tl, 36cl,
56tr, 61cr; Space Charts pages 28br, 32t; SPL page 26tr; Sally Bensusen (1988)/SPL page 9cr;
Tony Craddock/SPL page 57tr; David Ducros/SPL pages 29tc, 53cr; Geospace/SPL page 5tl;
Goddard Flight Control Center, Ken M. Johns/SPL page 56bl; David A. Hardy/SPL page
54tr; Tony and Daphne Hallas/SPL page 20tr; Ton Kinsbergen/SPL page 15cr; Max-Planck–
Institut fur Radioastronomie/SPL pages 6br, 25tr; Mehau Kulyk/SPL page 49bl; Naval
Research Laboratory/SPL page 7cr; Novosti Photo Library/SPL pages 32br, 34cl, 49tl; David
Parker/SPL page 25bl; Pekka Parviainen/SPL pages 15cr, 21tl; Rev. Ronald Royer/SPL
pages 15br, 23cr; Rosenfeld Images Ltd/SPL page 61cl; Royal Greenwich Observatory/SPL
page 24tl, 24cr; John Sanford/SPL page 4tl; Joe Tucciarone/SPL page 6cr; Dr Rudolph
Schild/SPL page 7bl; US Department of Energy/SPL page 62bl; D. Van Ravenswaay/SPL
page 21tr; TRH Pictures/NASM/NASA page 13br; TRH Pictures/NASA pages 18tr, 18cl,
33tl, 41tl; NASA/Image Select page 52br; Ann Ronan/Image Select page 28tl; Space
Frontiers page 33bl; TRH Pictures page 45tr; TRH Pictures/M. Roberts page 45br; The
Ronald Grant Archive page 50tl; University of Wisconsin Centre for Space Automation and
Robotics/SPL page 62br; SpaceShipOne courtesy of Scaled Composites, LLC/Mike Masse
page 60tr; US Air Force page 61br; Virgin Galactic pages 60cr, 60bl.

CONTENTS

WHAT IS SPACE LIKE?

LOOK up at the sky on a clear night and you will see the vastness of space, peppered with countless twinkling stars and planets. It looks as though it has been there forever, but once, a very long time ago, there was nothing. The universe did not exist. Most scientists believe that space and everything in it began about 13,800 million years ago with an enormous explosion called the Big Bang. Everything that exists came from the boiling soup of energy that poured out from the Big Bang. Most of the universe is empty, however. Matter is collected together in clumps to form stars and planets, and also in clouds where new stars are forming all the time. There is almost no matter at all in the empty tracts of space that lie between these clumps and clouds. There is no air in space and it is colder than the coldest place on Earth, unless you are near a star.

The night sky
As the sun sinks below the horizon each night and its light fades, the stars begin to appear. They cannot be seen during the day as the sun's light blocks them out. As your eyes become used to the darkness at night, more and more stars can be seen.

Galileo Galilei
The Italian scientist Galileo Galilei (1564-1642) was the first person to study the universe with a telescope. He saw mountains on the Earth's Moon and discovered moons orbiting the giant planet Jupiter. He also observed Saturn's rings, although he was unsure what they actually were. Galileo's many discoveries about the stars and planets made him famous all over Europe.

Telescope

Armillary sphere (represents the celestial sphere)

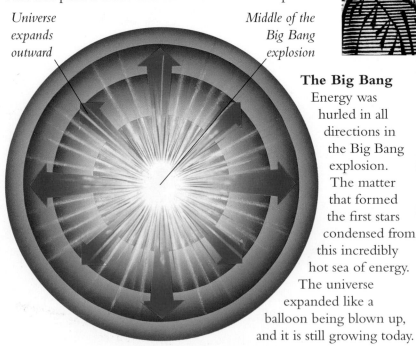

Universe expands outward

Middle of the Big Bang explosion

The Big Bang
Energy was hurled in all directions in the Big Bang explosion. The matter that formed the first stars condensed from this incredibly hot sea of energy. The universe expanded like a balloon being blown up, and it is still growing today.

Echoes of the Big Bang
In 1992, a space probe called COBE (COsmic Background Explorer) produced this sky-map. The pink, red and pale blue areas show variations in temperature left over from the Big Bang.

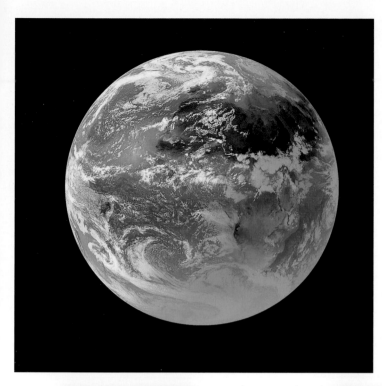

A jewel in space

The distinctive Earth stands out like a rare jewel against the blackness of space. The planet's blue oceans, green-carpeted land masses and swirling white clouds all combine to give it a unique appearance. The planet's abundant water and air also make the Earth the only known planet in the solar system capable of supporting life.

Layers of the atmosphere

Exosphere (upwards of 700km/435 miles)

Thermosphere (80–700km/ 50–435 miles)

Mesosphere (50–80km/ 31–50 miles)

Stratosphere (12–50km/ 7½–31 miles)

Troposphere (0–12km/ 0–7½ miles)

The Earth is surrounded by a blanket of air called the atmosphere. It is divided into five layers. The lowest layer, troposphere, is where the weather changes occur. It reaches a height of about 12km/ 7½ miles above the Earth. The stratosphere then reaches up to 50km/31 miles and the mesosphere extends to a height of 80km/50 miles. Above this are the thermosphere and exosphere layers. The air is so thin at this altitude that it fades away through these upper layers into space.

A human satellite

Astronaut Bruce McCandless hangs in space during a Space Shuttle flight in 1984, orbiting the Earth like the Moon or a satellite. He was testing an experimental one-man spacecraft called the Manned Manoeuvring Unit (MMU). He steered the MMU by using gas jets operated by hand controllers.

GALAXIES

S TARS are not spread evenly through space. They are clustered together in vast rotating groups called galaxies. One galaxy may contain thousands of millions of stars. Galaxies are so big that they are measured not in miles, but in light years. A light year is the distance light travels in a year, which is about 10 million million kilometres or 6 trillion miles. Galaxies are different shapes. Many are giant flat spirals, some are ball-shaped, while others seem to have no particular shape. We live in a spiral galaxy called the Milky Way. Many galaxies can be seen through telescopes. They look like fuzzy patches of light compared. The astronomer Charles Messier gave numbers to many galaxies. The Andromeda galaxy, for example, is also known by the Messier number M31.

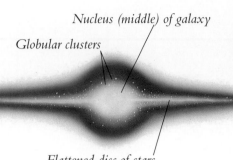

Nucleus (middle) of galaxy

Globular clusters

Flattened disc of stars

The Milky Way disc
Viewed from the side, the Milky Way looks like a thin, flat disc with a bulge in the middle. The disc is 3,000 light years thick, 100,000 light years across, and contains about 100 billion stars.

Above the Milky Way spiral
If you could look down on the Milky Way from above, you would see a beautiful spiral galaxy with glowing arms curling out into space. The Sun is a very ordinary star located between two major arms of the Milky Way. It is located about 30,000 light years away from the middle of the galaxy.

Make a spiral galaxy
Half-fill a 1-litre/1-quart jar with water. Use a paper punch to cut out about 20 paper circles. Carefully sprinkle the paper circles on the water, and then stir the water gently. See how the paper circles form a flattened rotating spiral, just like a spiral galaxy.

Radio astronomy
This is a radio picture of the Andromeda galaxy. Galaxies give out several forms of energy. Pictures can be made that show the types of energy. The colours in this image show the varying amounts of radio waves coming from different parts of Andromeda.

Elliptical galaxies
There are four main types of galaxy - elliptical, spiral, barred spiral and irregular. Elliptical galaxies are the most common, and may be ball-shaped or egg-shaped.

Spiral galaxies
A typical spiral galaxy is shaped like a flattened disc with a bulge in the middle, called the nucleus. The nucleus is surrounded by the curling spiral arms.

Barred spiral galaxies
A barred spiral is a type of spiral galaxy with an elongated, bar-shaped nucleus. Its spiral arms extend outwards from the ends of the bar.

Irregular galaxies
An irregular galaxy is unlike other galaxies as it has no particular shape. The Large Magellanic Cloud, one of the closest galaxies to Earth, is an irregular galaxy.

X-ray view of a galaxy
The High Energy Astronomy Observatory satellite HEAO-1 took this X-ray picture of the Milky Way in 1977. X-rays are the same sort of energy waves that doctors use when they need to look inside your body. False colours were added to the picture to show the many different sources of X-rays in the galaxy. The energy waves are given out by areas in space where large quantities of very hot gas are present. The temperature of the gas found in these areas can be as high as 1 million°C/1½ million°F.

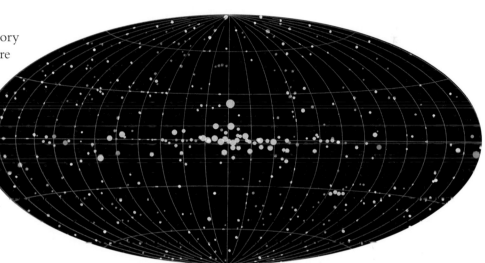

Middle of galaxy

M87 is an elliptical galaxy

Jet of plasma 5000 light years long

Galactic giant
A jet of particles shoots out from the middle of this false-colour image of the M87 galaxy. M87 is so big that light takes 40,000 years to cross it. The galaxy is surrounded by hundreds of clumps of stars called globular clusters, each of which contains about a million stars.

FACT BOX

• The biggest known galaxy is about six million light years across. It is located about one billion light years away in the constellation Serpens.

• The most distant galaxies found so far are more than 13,000 million light years away from Earth.

• The Milky Way belongs to a collection of about 30 galaxies called the Local Group. These galaxies move through space together.

WHAT IS A STAR?

A STAR is a giant ball of gas. Most of it is hydrogen, the lightest gas of all. At the core, particles of matter smash into each other with such incredible force that they fuse together, releasing a burst of energy. This is called nuclear fusion. Most stars can release energy steadily for thousands of millions of years. Stars are formed in giant clouds of dust and gas called nebulae. Clumps of matter inside a nebula attract more and more matter towards them. Each clump grows bigger and bigger until nuclear fusion starts. The nuclear reactions create heat and light, and the star begins to shine. It burns brightly for thousands of millions of years, until no more hydrogen is left. Small stars then shrink to become white dwarfs. Large stars change into objects called neutron stars. The biggest stars become the strangest objects in the Universe – black holes.

Stellar birthplace
The Orion Nebula is the birthplace for hundreds of stars. It is a vast cloud of dust and gas in which new stars are forming. When viewed through a telescope, the cloud appears to glow brightly. It is illuminated by the many stars that have already formed inside it.

How a star forms

1. Clumps of dust and gas inside a nebula condense to form spinning objects called protostars.

2. Each protostar becomes very tightly packed and attracts more dust and gas towards it by gravity.

3. Nuclear fusion begins, pouring out energy and blowing away surrounding gas and dust.

4. The remaining dust and gas form a flattened disc of matter orbiting around the star.

5. The disc of debris may eventually form planets and moons, as it did around our own star, the Sun.

6. The star begins to shine as hydrogen atoms in its core join to form helium.

Supernova remnant
This false-colour photograph shows the light energy given off by the Crab Nebula. A nebula is a cloud of gas and dust thrown out into space when a massive star explodes. The explosion is also known as a supernova. Chinese astronomers recorded the explosion that formed the Crab Nebula when it took place in 1054. The supernova was bright enough to be seen during daylight hours. The remains of the star can be seen at the centre of the false-colour picture. The colours run from red for the brightest regions of the nebula and fade to yellow, green, blue and silver.

Life cycle of an average-size star

Most stars change hydrogen into helium for thousands of millions of years. This period is called the main sequence. When an average-size star like the Sun runs out of hydrogen, it does not explode in a supernova like a massive star. Instead, it begins converting helium into carbon and expands into a red giant. When the helium runs out, the star ejects its outer layers. It then shrinks, becoming a white dwarf. Finally, the white dwarf cools to become a black dwarf.

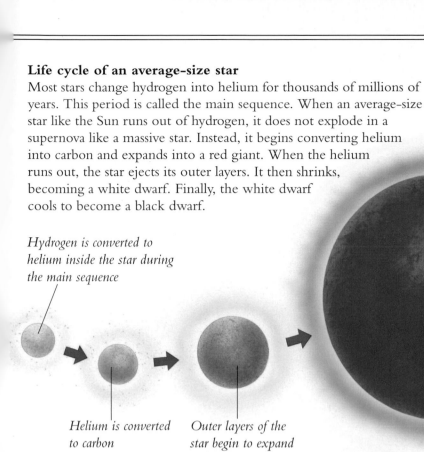

Hydrogen is converted to helium inside the star during the main sequence

Helium is converted to carbon

Outer layers of the star begin to expand

Black dwarf

White dwarf

Outer layers of the star are thrown off

The star becomes a red giant

Types of stars

Stars are classified according to how hot they are. Generally, the more material a star has, the higher its temperature. The hottest stars are blue while the coolest are reddish brown. The chart below gives a selection of star types and temperatures.

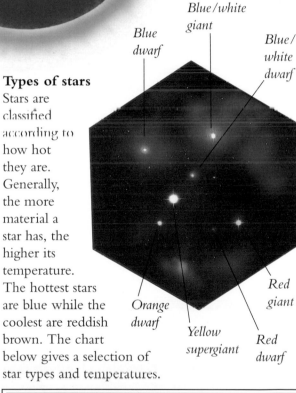

Blue dwarf

Blue/white giant

Blue/white dwarf

Orange dwarf

Yellow supergiant

Red giant

Red dwarf

Star types	Class	Temperature	Example
Violet	O	Over 28,000°C/50,000°F	10 Lacertae
Hottest blue stars	B	10,000–28,000°C/18,000–50,000°F	Rigel
Blue star	A	7,500–10,000°C/13,500–18,000°F	Sirius
Blue/white	F	6,000–7,500°C/10,800–13,500°F	Canopus
White/yellow	G	5,000–6,000°C/9,000–10,800°F	The Sun
Orange/red	K	3,500–5,000°C/6,300–9,000°F	Arcturus
Red	M	Less than 3,500°C/6,300°F	Betelgeuse

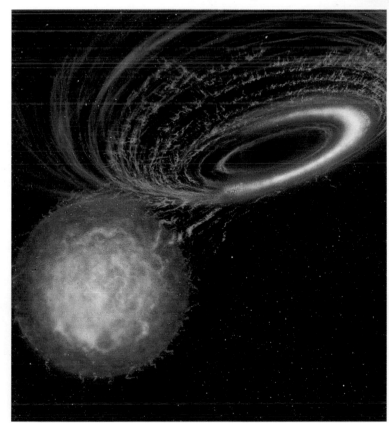

Holes in space

Stellar matter spirals into a black hole. When a massive star explodes, the dense, collapsed core that is left generates a strong gravitational field. A black hole is formed when the field is so strong that it bends space into an invisible one-way funnel. Not even light can escape from the black hole's pull of gravity.

PULSARS AND BLACK HOLES

Pulsars and black holes are two of the strangest types of objects in the Universe. Pulsars are spinning objects that send out regular pulses of radio energy. They are formed from the collapsed cores of exploded stars that were originally six to eight times the size of the Sun. A pulsar sends out a narrow beam of radio waves as it sweeps around the sky. As the pulsar is rotating, the radio beam appears to flash on and off, like the light from a light-house. Black holes are produced when even bigger stars explode. The core that is left cools, as nuclear reactions are no longer taking place to produce heat. This reduces the pressure pushing outwards from within the star. Gravity pulls the star's material towards its middle. If the force of gravity is strong enough, the star continues to shrink until it is no longer visible. It has become a black hole. Follow these projects to make a flashing pulsar and to demonstrate how a black hole forms.

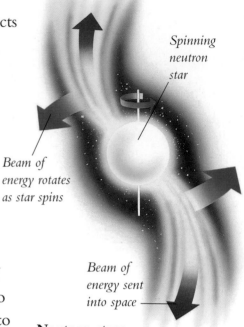

Spinning neutron star

Beam of energy rotates as star spins

Beam of energy sent into space

Neutron stars
As the core of an exploded massive star collapses, it begins to spin rapidly. The core is also called a neutron star, as it is made from tightly packed neutron particles. Pulsars are spinning neutron stars that send out energy pulses many times per second. The types of energy sent out include light, X-rays and radio waves.

MAKE A PULSAR

You will need: ruler, string, scissors, door frame, sticky tape, torch (flashlight).

1 Measure out 60cm/24in of string using a ruler. Cut the string with scissors. Tie or tape one end of the string to a door frame. Be careful not to damage the frame's surface.

2 Wrap the other end of the string around the middle of the torch. Tie it in a knot. Tape the string to the torch to secure it. Make sure that the torch can spin around freely.

3 With the curtains closed and the lights off, spin the torch around. As the light sweeps around the room, it appears to blink on and off like a pulsar's radio beams.

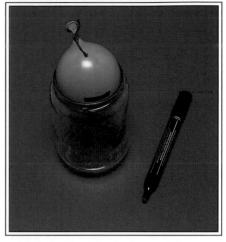

1 Place one of the jars on top of a work surface. Attach a round balloon to a balloon pump. Dangle the balloon so that half of it is inside the jar and half of it is outside.

2 Blow up the balloon. Ask a friend to tie a piece of string around the balloon's neck to keep the air in. Now repeat steps 1 and 2 with the second balloon and jar.

3 Using a permanent marker pen, carefully mark a line on each balloon along the top of each jar. Make sure you do not press too hard, as this may burst the balloons.

FORMING A BLACK HOLE

You will need:
2 large-mouthed glass jars,
2 small round balloons,
balloon pump, string,
permanent marker pen.

Entrance to black hole

One-way trip
A black hole bends space into a deep funnel. Nearby matter is sucked in, disappearing altogether from the Universe.

Funnel of black hole

4 Put one jar, with the balloon half inside and half outside, in a freezer. After 30 minutes remove the jar and balloon. The balloon has sunk into the jar, as shown.

5 Compare the chilled balloon with the balloon that has remained at room temperature. The chilled balloon has sunk into its jar, but the other balloon has not. As the air particles inside the chilled balloon grew colder, they packed closer together, reducing the pressure inside the balloon. This caused the stretchy rubber to shrink, like a star's core collapsing under its own gravity to form a black hole.

CONSTELLATIONS

URING the night, stars seem to rise and set as the Earth rotates. As the months go by, new stars come into view as the Earth moves in its orbit around the sun. People have looked at the night sky and spotted patterns in the stars for thousands of years. Finding patterns made it easier to follow the movements of the stars across the sky. In ancient times few people had written calendars. Instead they followed the passing of time by looking at the movements of stars. It was important to know when certain stars appeared in the sky, because they marked the times when crops should be planted or harvested, or when migrating animals would return and could be killed for food. In the ancient world, people named groups of stars after the heroes and creatures of their legends. The ancient Greeks divided the stars into 48 groups called constellations, 12 of which form the signs of the Zodiac. Another 40 constellations have since been added, making a total of 88.

Star patterns
The Big Dipper (also called the Plough) is a familiar sight in the sky in the Northern Hemisphere. It is formed from seven stars in Ursa Major (Great Bear). Ursa Major is one of the oldest constellations and is easy to find in the sky.

North Celestial Pole

Stars appear to be fixed to the inside of the rotating sphere

Earth's equator

Constellation

Celestial sphere appears to spin around the poles

Celestial equator

Celestial sphere
As the Earth moves around the sun on its yearly orbit, different sections of the sky come into view. This creates the illusion that the Earth is surrounded by an enormous, hollow rotating sphere, the inside of which is studded with all the stars. Astronomers find the concept of the celestial sphere useful, as it helps them locate the position of objects in the sky.

South Celestial Pole

Aquarius
The Helix Nebula is found within Aquarius.

Taurus
The Crab Nebula is located within the constellation of Taurus.

Cancer
This faint constellation contains the M44 and M67 star clusters.

Capricorn
The brightest star in Capricorn is the binary star Alpha Capricorni.

Pisces
This constellation contains the spiral galaxy M74.

Aries
The double star Gamma Arietis is found in Aries.

Scorpio
The red supergiant Antares lies within Scorpio.

Leo
The spiral galaxies M65 and M66 are located in Leo.

Virgo
The constellation of Virgo contains the Sombrero galaxy, M104.

Sagittarius
The heart of the Milky Way galaxy lies behind the constellation of Sagittarius.

Gemini
The bright stars of Castor and Pollux are located in Gemini.

Libra
The constellation of Libra is a faint, kite-shaped galaxy.

The Zodiac
As the sun, the planets and their moons move through space, their positions in the sky as seen from Earth change. They follow an imaginary path in the sky called the ecliptic, which passes through 12 constellations. These constellations are called the Zodiac. The constellations of the Zodiac are used by astronomers to help identify parts of the sky.

Stellar distances
The stars that make up a constellation such as Orion (shown here) appear to be close together. This is because they lie in the same direction when seen from Earth. Some of Orion's stars are much closer to us than others. If you could look at Orion from somewhere else in the galaxy, it would look completely different.

- Orion Nebula
- Mintaka
- Rigel
- Betelgeuse
- Alnitak
- Saiph
- Alnilam
- Bellatrix

Each division equals 500 light years

Orion as it appears from Earth

Bright as a galaxy
These quasars (quasi-stellar objects) look like stars as they are so far away, but each one is as bright as a whole galaxy. Astronomers believe that quasars may be the cores of incredibly bright galaxies.

THE SUN, OUR STAR

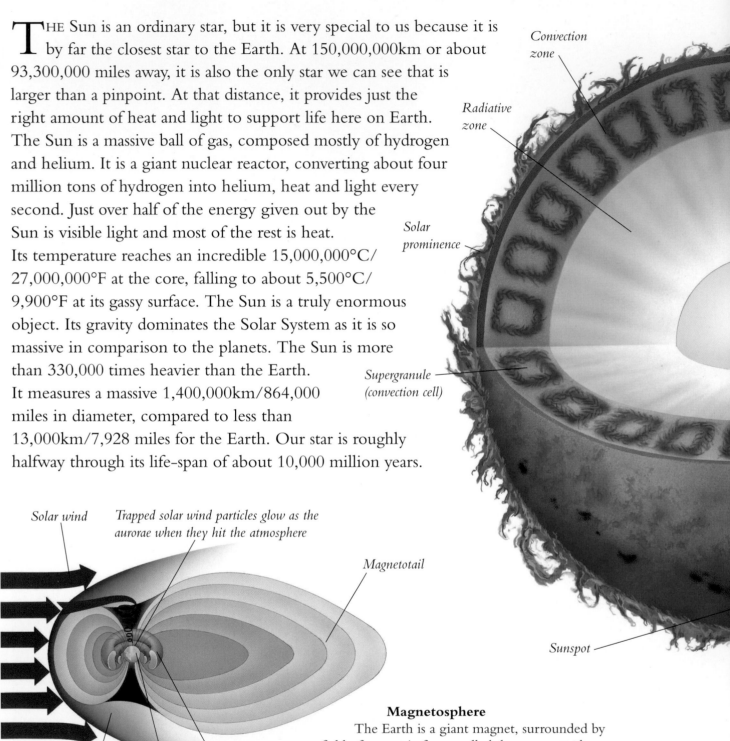

THE Sun is an ordinary star, but it is very special to us because it is by far the closest star to the Earth. At 150,000,000km or about 93,300,000 miles away, it is also the only star we can see that is larger than a pinpoint. At that distance, it provides just the right amount of heat and light to support life here on Earth. The Sun is a massive ball of gas, composed mostly of hydrogen and helium. It is a giant nuclear reactor, converting about four million tons of hydrogen into helium, heat and light every second. Just over half of the energy given out by the Sun is visible light and most of the rest is heat. Its temperature reaches an incredible 15,000,000°C/ 27,000,000°F at the core, falling to about 5,500°C/ 9,900°F at its gassy surface. The Sun is a truly enormous object. Its gravity dominates the Solar System as it is so massive in comparison to the planets. The Sun is more than 330,000 times heavier than the Earth. It measures a massive 1,400,000km/864,000 miles in diameter, compared to less than 13,000km/7,928 miles for the Earth. Our star is roughly halfway through its life-span of about 10,000 million years.

Convection zone

Radiative zone

Solar prominence

Supergranule (convection cell)

Sunspot

Solar wind

Trapped solar wind particles glow as the aurorae when they hit the atmosphere

Magnetotail

The magnetosphere acts as a buffer between the Earth's upper atmosphere and the solar wind

The Earth

The Van Allen radiation belts are located above the Earth's equator

Magnetosphere

The Earth is a giant magnet, surrounded by a field of magnetic forces called the magnetosphere. This field stretches far out into space. The Sun sends out streams of particles called solar wind, which squeeze the Earth's magnetosphere on the side nearest the Sun. This gives the magnetosphere an elongated teardrop shape. The long magnetotail on the side of the Earth facing away from the Sun can stretch as far as the Moon's orbit.

Core
(15,000,000°C/27,000,000°F)

Photosphere
(5,500°C/9,900°F)

Aurora borealis
Solar wind particles raining down on the Earth's poles produce spectacular coloured lights in the sky. These are called aurorae. An aurora at the North Pole *(shown left)* is called an aurora borealis. An aurora appearing at the South Pole is called an aurora australis.

Solar probe
In 1995, the SOHO space probe (SOlar and Heliospheric Observatory) was launched to study the Sun. It orbits the Sun 1,500,000km/930,000 miles from Earth, at a point where the Sun's pull of gravity exactly balances the pull of the Earth. Space probes like SOHO warn scientists when Earth's magnetosphere might be affected by solar storms.

Inside the Sun
The stormy surface of the Sun boils furiously as energy pours out from its core. Curling tongues of fiery gas bigger than the Earth are often flung out into space. These are called solar prominences. Dark spots called sunspots often appear on the Sun's surface. They are caused by magnetic disturbances within the star. Sunspots are areas of cooler gas that appear to be black in contrast to their hotter, brighter surroundings.

FACT BOX

• The Sun creates energy at the same rate as a million million hydrogen bombs exploding each second!

• The number of sunspots on the Sun's surface reaches a peak every 11 years.

• The Sun is 30,000 light years from the centre of the Milky Way galaxy.

• The Sun takes roughly 25 days to make one rotation at the equator. At the poles it rotates more slowly, taking about 35 days to make one rotation.

Solar eclipse
When the Moon's orbit causes it to pass directly between the Earth and the Sun, a total solar eclipse occurs. With the Sun's blinding light blocked out by the Moon, the star's gassy outer atmosphere, called the corona, can be clearly seen.

ORBITS AND DISTANCES

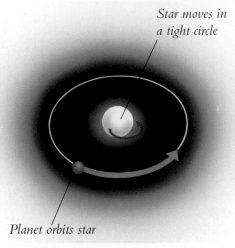

Star moves in a tight circle

Planet orbits star

Wobbling star

A planet's gravity pulls the star it orbits around in a tight circle, making the star appear to wobble. Planets orbiting distant stars are too small to be seen, but by looking for this telltale wobble astronomers have detected stars that may have planets.

S OLAR systems and galaxies are held together by the invisible force of gravity generated by stars, planets and other stellar bodies. Gravity causes moons to orbit (circle) around planets, planets to orbit stars, and stars to orbit the core of the galaxy. An orbit is a balancing act. A star's gravity pulls a planet towards it. This is balanced by the planet's natural tendency to travel in a straight line rather than circling around the star. Try making your own modelling-clay planet orbiting a modelling-clay star. In your model, the star's gravitational pull is simulated by the downward pull on a piece of string of the clay star. Constellations of stars are not held together by gravity in the same way as solar systems. The stars in a constellation such as Orion appear to be close together as they lie in the same direction when seen from Earth. By making a model of Orion you can see that its shape and the distance between its stars would look very different from elsewhere in the galaxy.

Orbiting planet

Star

MAKE A PLANET ORBITING A STAR

You will need: string, scissors, ballpoint pen barrel, paper clips, modelling clay.

1 Cut a piece of string to about 45cm/18in in length. Thread the piece of string through the ballpoint pen barrel. Tie a paper clip to each end of the string.

2 Divide the modelling clay into two lumps, one twice the size of the other. Roll each lump of clay into a ball. Push a paper clip into each ball, as shown.

3 Hold the pen barrel, with the large ball (star) supported by your hand. Spin the small ball (planet) in a circle. Let go of the large ball. The downward pull of the star balances the centripetal (spinning) force of the planet, keeping it in a stable orbit.

MAKE A MODEL OF ORION

1 Cut out 2 pieces of cardboard, each measuring 10cm x 6cm/ 4in x 2¼in. Then cut out 2 pieces measuring 24cm x 6cm/9½in x 2¼in, and 1 piece measuring 10cm x 24cm/4in x 9½in.

2 Using the black marker pen and a ruler, draw a grid of 1cm/½in squares on the 10cm x 24cm/4 x 9½in card. The 10cm/4in edge forms an X axis. The 24cm/9½in edge forms a Y axis.

3 Tape the card pieces together to form a box. Mark the X axis with an X and number the squares from 1 to 10. Mark the Y axis with a Y and number from 1 to 24.

You will need: cardboard, ruler, scissors, marker pens (red and black), sticky tape, wooden skewers, modelling clay.

Star	X axis	Y axis	Length
Betelgeuse	1cm (½in)	6cm (2¼in)	17.5cm (6¾in)
Bellatrix	7cm (2¾in)	4.5cm (1¾in)	16.5cm (6½in)
Alnitak	4cm (1¾in)	18cm (7in)	9.5cm (3¾in)
Alnilam	5cm (2in)	18cm (7in)	10cm (4in)
Mintaka	6cm (2¼in)	18cm (7in)	10cm (4in)
Saiph	2.5cm (1in)	21cm (8⅓in)	3cm (1¼in)
Rigel	9.5cm (3¾in)	10cm (4in)	4.5cm (1¾in)

Familiar stars

The three bright stars that form Orion's belt stand out very clearly, making it easy to spot. Orion can be seen from both the northern and southern hemispheres of the Earth.

4 Using the red marker pen, mark 7 wooden skewers 6cm/2¼in from the point. Cut them to the lengths shown in the table and attach a clay star to each end.

5 Using the X and Y co-ordinates for each star shown in the table, push the skewers through the top of the box. Make sure they are pushed through up to the red marks.

6 To view Orion as it is seen from Earth, position the box as shown above. If you look at the model from the side, the constellation will form a completely different shape.

THE SOLAR SYSTEM

THE Solar System is made up of the Sun, the planets, their moons and every other object that is influenced by the Sun's gravity. It was created about 4,600 million years ago from a cloud of dust and gas. Its formation may have been triggered by an exploding star nearby. Eight planets follow endless orbits around the Sun, trapped by its invisible but immensely powerful pull of gravity. The inner planets of Mercury, Venus, Earth and Mars are small rocky worlds, while most of the outer planets (Jupiter, Saturn, Uranus and Neptune) are giants made mainly from gas and liquid. Until 2006, the solar system had nine planets. The ninth planet was Pluto, a tiny world orbiting the Sun far beyond the giant planet Neptune. When astronomers found more worlds like Pluto, they decided to call Pluto and these new worlds dwarf planets. So, Pluto was not a planet any more and the solar system now has eight planets.

Saturn's rings
The beautiful rings of the planet Saturn are actually made of countless pieces of rock and ice. They form a flat disc around the planet's equator and range in size from tiny particles of dust to lumps the size of a house.

Volcanoes on Mars
Space probes have found volcanoes on several planets in the Solar System and at least one moon. This clay model shows Olympus Mons on Mars, the largest known volcano in the Solar System. It is 500km/310 miles across and reaches a height of 25km/16 miles. Olympus Mons is about three times as high as Earth's tallest mountain, Mount Everest.

Mercury orbits the Sun once every 88 days, only 58,000,000km/ 36 million miles away from its searing heat. The tiny planet roasts on one side and freezes on the other.

Venus is a hot-house planet covered by thick clouds. It appears in the sky as a bright star.

Earth is the largest of the rocky inner planets. Most of its surface is covered by water.

Mars is also known as the Red Planet, as it is covered by red dust. Its surface often disappears under fierce dust storms. The planet has polar ice caps made from frozen carbon dioxide that grow and shrink with the changing seasons.

THE SUN

Planets' relative distance from the Sun (below)

Merc. Venus Earth Mars   Jupiter   Saturn   Uranus

- About 60 per cent of Mercury's surface is covered with craters made by meteorite impacts.

- The atmospheric pressure on the surface of Venus is 90 times that of the Earth at sea level.

- Saturn is a giant planet, but it is so light that it would float on water.

In the blink of an eye

Scientists believe that the Solar System formed from a cloud of gas and dust in a relatively short time. It probably took about 100 million years from the moment the cloud started to collapse until the Sun burst into fiery life. This may seem to be a very long time in human terms, but compared to the age of the Universe it is a mere blink of a cosmic eye.

Pluto is one of countless millions of icy worlds that belong to a swarm of distant bodies called the Kuiper Belt. Pluto is the largest Kuiper Belt object found so far.

Neptune is a hazy blue world. Like Uranus, Neptune is made of water, ammonia and methane, unlike Jupiter and Saturn, which are made mainly of hydrogen and helium. One of Neptune's 13 moons, Triton, is almost as big as Earth's moon.

The planet Uranus is tipped over on its side. The green-blue planet is a gas giant, like Jupiter. It takes 84 years to orbit the Sun. It looks the same all over, as its hazy atmosphere receives little heat from the Sun or from inside the planet.

The Great Red Spot

Ammonia clouds

Saturn is surrounded by a system of broad flat rings. About every 14 years the rings are tilted so that they are seen edge-on from Earth.

Jovian hurricane

Jupiter's Great Red Spot is a massive hurricane-like storm. It is 40,000km/25,000 miles long by 11,000km/6,800 miles wide. Three planets the size of the Earth could fit along its length. The storm has been raging for centuries. It may have been observed as early as 1665 by the Italian astronomer Giovanni Domenico Cassini.

The gas giant Jupiter is the biggest planet in the Solar System. It has a mass two and a half times greater than all the other planets put together. Jupiter rotates very quickly – once every 10 hours. Its four largest moons, discovered by Galileo, can be seen with a pair of binoculars. Jupiter has 67 moons in total.

Neptune

Pluto and other Kuiper Belt objects

COMETS AND METEORS

CHUNKS of rock, ice and dust left over from the formation of the Solar System still orbit the Sun today. Some of them are asteroids that range from microscopic grains of dust to pieces of rock almost as large as small planets. It is thought that lumps of ice and rock orbit the Sun far beyond the most distant planet. Collisions and the pull of gravity from the outer planets sometimes draw one of them in towards the Sun. As it nears the Sun, dust and gas are driven off it and swept back into a tail, forming a comet. Sunlight reflects off the dust, and the gas glows. Some comets follow an orbit that brings them back within sight of the Earth at regular intervals. The most famous of these is Halley's Comet. When a meteoroid (a grain of space dust) travels into the Earth's atmosphere from space, it is heated so much by friction (rubbing) with the air that it glows and turns to vapour. This forms a shooting star, or meteor. A larger piece of rock that is big enough to reach the ground before it burns up is called a meteorite.

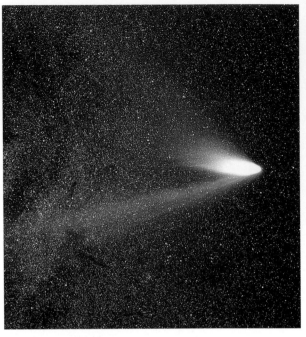

Comet Hale-Bopp
This comet was discovered by astronomers Alan Hale and Thomas Bopp in 1995. The last time the comet's orbit brought it in range of the Earth was 4,000 years ago. Since then, the gravitational pull of the planets has changed its orbit. As a result, it will next pass the Earth in about 2,380 years.

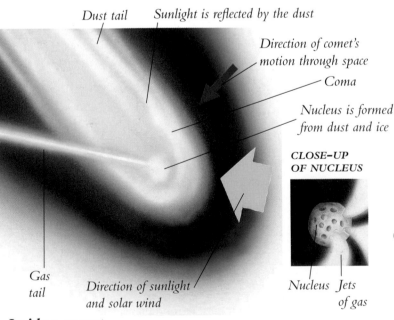

Dust tail — Sunlight is reflected by the dust

Direction of comet's motion through space

Coma

Nucleus is formed from dust and ice

CLOSE-UP OF NUCLEUS

Gas tail

Direction of sunlight and solar wind

Nucleus   Jets of gas

Inside a comet
The solid part of a comet is called its nucleus. The fuzzy ball that we see is a cloud of gas and dust, called the coma, that surrounds the comet's nucleus. As it nears the Sun, the solar wind and sunlight sweep some of the coma back into a tail.

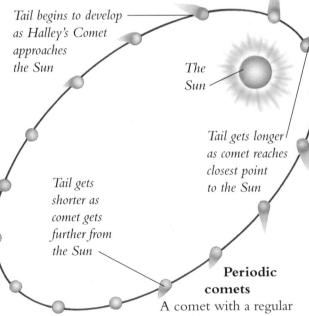

Tail begins to develop as Halley's Comet approaches the Sun

The Sun

Tail gets longer as comet reaches closest point to the Sun

Tail gets shorter as comet gets further from the Sun

Periodic comets
A comet with a regular orbit that brings it close to the Sun is called a periodic comet. Halley's Comet, for example, orbits the Sun every 76 years. When it last returned in 1986, the space probe *Giotto* flew close by it and took pictures of the comet's nucleus.

Types of meteorite

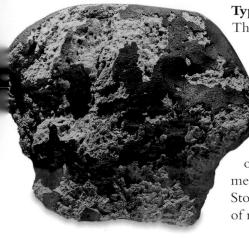

This meteorite is made of rock. There are three main types of meteorite – irons, stony and stony irons. Irons are made of metal. Stony meteorites are rocky. Stony irons are a mix of rock and metal.

Fireworks in the sky

A shower of meteors streak through the sky. Meteor showers take place when the Earth's orbit takes it through debris left behind by passing comets. The dust and rock burn up in the atmosphere, creating a spectacular firework display.

The biggest meteorites create the deepest craters

Smaller meteorites make shallower craters

Making meteor craters

Fill a deep tray or bowl with sand. Drop balls of different sizes and weights into the tray and see how they make craters. Experiment to see the different types of crater formed when you drop the balls at different angles and speeds.

Impact with the Earth

When a large meteorite hits the ground, it gouges out a crater. Meteor Crater in Arizona, USA, is 1,200m/3,900ft across and was created when an iron meteorite weighing 25 tons hit the ground 50,000 years ago. Most craters on Earth are worn away over time by wind and water.

Space rock

Asteroid 243 Ida is a typical asteroid. It is a jagged chunk of dust-covered space rock, measuring 52km/32 miles in length. The asteroid's dusty surface is pitted with craters caused by collisions with other asteroids and meteoroids.

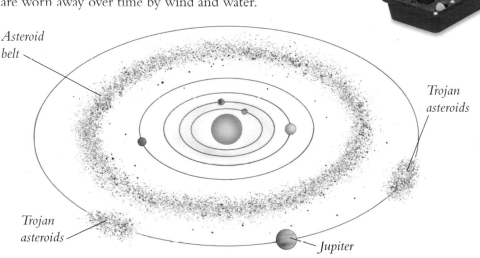

Asteroid belt

Trojan asteroids

Trojan asteroids

Jupiter

The asteroid belt

Millions of asteroids lie in a broad belt between the orbits of Mars and Jupiter. The largest, Ceres, is 940km/584 miles across. It was the first to be discovered, in 1801. The orbits of more than 5,000 asteroids are now known. Two more groups of asteroids, called the Trojans, share the same orbit as Jupiter.

SOLAR HEAT AND WIND

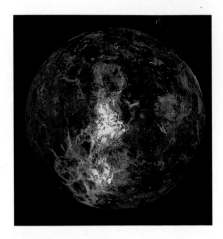

Hot-house planet
This picture shows Venus without its thick cloud layers, revealing the planet's scorched surface. Mercury is the closest planet to the Sun, but Venus has a higher surface temperature. This is because its dense cloud layer traps more of the Sun's heat, like a greenhouse.

NEARLY half of the energy given out by the Sun is heat. Infra-red (heat) rays produced by the Sun travel away from the star into space. Anything that the rays hit absorbs them and becomes warmer. As the rays get further away from the Sun, they spread out and their heating power weakens. You can see this effect yourself by carrying out a simple heating experiment with a lamp, a metre rule (yardstick) and two thermometers. The Sun also sends out a fast-moving stream of particles called the solar wind. This effect can be observed when a comet approaches the Sun. The streams of solar wind particles carry gas from the comet backwards to form a tail. As the comet approaches the Sun, the tail stretches out behind it. However, as the comet travels away from the Sun, it moves tail first. The fast stream of particles sent out by the Sun ensure that the tail of the comet is always pointing away from the star. You can demonstrate how the solar wind produces a comet's long gas-tail by performing a simple but effective experiment that uses paint, water and a tray.

HEATING PLANETS

You will need:
1m ruler (yardstick),
2 thermometers,
desk lamp.

1 Lay the ruler on the ground. Place one thermometer at 10cm/4in and the other at 100cm/40in. Place the lamp at the 0cm/0in end of the ruler.

2 Adjust the lamp so it shines on the thermometer at 10cm/4in. Turn on the lamp. After 10-15 minutes, compare the two thermometers.

3 The thermometer closer to the lamp is hotter. Similarly, planets closest to the Sun are heated more than those that are farther away.

MAKE A COMET

You will need: small tray, plastic bowl, paint, paintbrush, watering can, water.

1 Take the tray and place it on end in the bowl. Make sure that the underside of the tray faces forwards so that water can run freely over it.

2 Dip the paintbrush in the paint. Carefully place a thick blob of the paint at the top of the tray, roughly in the middle.

3 Fill the watering can with water. Gently pour the water over the top of the paint blob comet. The paint streams away from the comet, creating a long tail behind the blob nucleus. The water behaves like the solar wind, sweeping gas from the comet back to form a long gas-tail.

Nucleus of comet

Tail of comet

A tale of two tails
Comet West streaks past the Earth, displaying its spectacular glowing tails. Comets can have one or two tails. This depends on what the comet is made from and how close it approaches the Sun. When Comet West passed by the Earth in 1976, it had a glowing white dust-tail and a blue gas-tail.

ASTRONOMY

THE scientific study of the Universe is called astronomy. Astronomers use telescopes to help them study the stars. Optical telescopes use either lenses or mirrors to make distant objects look bigger and brighter. Lens telescopes are also called refractors, while mirror telescopes are called reflectors. Most large astronomical telescopes are reflectors. Telescopes are often built on top of mountains, where the thin, clear air and dark skies give the best views. Stars give out other types of energy as well as light, including radio waves. The Earth's atmosphere stops some types of star energy, such as X-rays, from reaching the ground. X-ray telescopes have to be launched into space, so that they can be used outside the atmosphere.

View from a volcano
The William Herschel Telescope (WHT) is located 2,400m/7,800ft above sea level on top of an extinct volcano on La Palma, in the Canary Islands. The high altitude provides an excellent view of the stars.

ESO Telescope
The European Southern Observatory (ESO) New Technology Telescope (NTT) is one of 15 astronomical instruments at La Silla observatory in Chile. Its main mirror is 3.58m/11¾ft across. The NTT first began operating in 1989. Its performance was improved with an upgrade in 1997.

Lightweight skeleton frame

Primary mirror

Motors adjust position of telescope

Moving mirror
The WHT's giant 4.2m/13¾ft-diameter primary mirror is given a final polishing using a special machine. It is one of the most accurately shaped mirrors in the world.

Radio dish antenna

Cameras and instruments housed inside HST

Solar panels provide electricity

Aperture door

Hubble Space Telescope
In 1990, the Space Shuttle launched the Hubble Space Telescope (HST) into orbit around the Earth. It is an optical telescope that measures 13.3m/44ft in length and 4.2m/14ft across. Solar panels provide it with power. The HST weighs nearly 11 tons and orbits the Earth at a height of 570km/354 miles. It sends its images back to Earth by radio.

Linking telescopes

The Very Large Array (VLA) points skywards. The VLA is a group of 27 movable radio telescopes in New Mexico, USA. Each dish measures 25m/82ft across. The dishes are linked together so that they behave like parts of one huge dish.

Arecibo radio telescope

The world's biggest radio telescope is built in a natural hollow in the ground near the city of Arecibo in Puerto Rico. The Arecibo dish is 305m/1,000ft across and is fixed in position. To scan the sky, motors steer the receiver suspended above the dish.

Radio pictures

This image shows radio energy from the Milky Way. Radio telescopes measure the strength of radio energy coming from different points in the sky. The energy strength at each point can be turned into brightness. False colours are added to make a vivid picture.

Dear ET...

In 1974, this message was transmitted into the depths of space using the Arecibo radio telescope. It contains a simple representation of a human being, and was directed at a star cluster in the constellation of Hercules. It also shows the location of the Solar System within the Milky Way galaxy. If intelligent alien creatures ever receive and process the transmission, they should be able to understand where the message came from. They should also be able to work out what sort of beings sent it.

FACT BOX

• The Kepler space telescope was launched in 2009 to search for Earth-like planets orbiting other stars. By 2013 it had found 132. Scientists will be working on its discoveries for many years to come.

• The Spitzer space telescope was launched in 2003 to search for objects by detecting the heat they give out. It could see through dark dust and find stars forming behind it.

LOOKING INTO SPACE

Greenwich Observatory
The Royal Observatory in Greenwich, England, was founded by King Charles II in 1675. The King paid for the buildings, but the astronomer had to buy his own telescopes!

OPTICAL telescopes work by bending light rays, making objects appear closer and larger than is actually the case. They bend light in two different ways. Refracting telescopes use lenses. Light rays from distant objects change direction as they enter the lens and again as they leave it. There are difficulties involved in making very big lenses, so most of the telescopes used in astronomy are of the reflecting type. These telescopes use mirrors instead of lenses. A reflecting telescope's main mirror is curved, so that light rays hitting it bounce off at an angle. Our brains work out how big an object is by analyzing the angle of the light rays from it as the rays enter our eyes. Telescopes use lenses or mirrors to change this angle, fooling our brain into thinking that the light has come from a much bigger object. You can see how both refracting telescopes and reflecting telescopes work by carrying out these simple experiments using lenses and mirrors.

MAKE A SINGLE-MIRROR REFLECTING TELESCOPE

You will need: desk lamp, thick purple paper, marker pen, scissors, sticky tape, small mirror, magnifying glass, modelling clay.

Starlight   Eyepiece lens   Primary mirror reflects an upside-down image

Secondary mirror corrects image

Reflecting telescope
Light reflects off the primary mirror. The light rays bounce off a small secondary mirror and are focused and magnified by an eyepiece lens.

1 Draw a circle around the front of the lamp on a sheet of purple paper. Cut it out. Then cut out a central arrow *(shown left)*. Stick the circle on to the front of the lamp.

2 Set up the desk lamp and mirror so that the mirror reflects the light from the lamp on to a nearby wall. Use modelling clay to help support the mirror, if necessary.

3 Set up the magnifying glass so that light reflecting from the mirror passes through it. The lens magnifies and focuses the light, projecting an upside-down arrow.

MAKE A REFRACTING TELESCOPE

1 Draw around the front of the desk lamp on a sheet of red paper. Using scissors, cut out a star in the middle of the circle. Then cut out the circle, as shown.

2 Using sticky tape, fasten the circle of paper securely over the front of the desk lamp. Make sure that it does not touch the bulb, as this could cause the paper to burn.

3 Position the desk lamp so that it shines on a nearby wall. Adjust the angle of the lamp if necessary. Make sure that the lamp's base is stable to prevent it overbalancing.

You will need:
desk lamp, thick red
paper, marker pen,
scissors, sticky tape,
2 magnifying glasses,
modelling clay.

Starlight   *Focal point*   *Eyepiece lens*

Objective lens

Refracting telescopes
Light from a distant star passes through the objective lens. This forms a magnified, blurry image of the star. The image is brought into focus by the lens in the eyepiece.

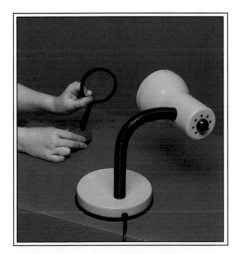

4 Position a magnifying glass between the lamp and the wall. To support the glass and fix it in place, take the handle and wedge it firmly in a lump of modelling clay.

5 Turn on the lamp. Adjust the magnifying glass so that the light passing through it appears as a blurred patch of light. The glass acts like a telescope's objective lens.

6 Position the second lens behind the first lens. This acts as an eyepiece lens. Adjust the eyepiece lens until the light is focused to form the sharp image of the star.

ROCKET PROPULSION

Visions of the future
In the late 1800s, the French writer Jules Verne (1828-1905) wrote imaginative stories about the future. He predicted space travel many years before the first aircraft flew in 1903.

ROCKET engines are the only motors powerful enough to lift a heavy spacecraft into orbit and beyond. The earliest rocket propulsion worked by burning a solid fuel. This type of rocket is not suitable for spaceflight because it cannot be controlled – the fuel simply burns until there is none left. Solid fuel booster rockets were used to provide extra power during the lift-off of the Space Shuttle and are still used by some rockets. For spaceflight itself, a controllable rocket is usually needed. This type of engine can be turned on and off and varied in power like the engine of a car. Liquid fuel rockets are used for spaceflight as they can be controlled in this way. They produce a stream of searing hot gas from the engine nozzle, usually by burning a mixture of liquefied oxygen and liquid hydrogen fuel in a combustion chamber. The gases rushing out in one direction create a huge amount of thrust, pushing the rocket in the opposite direction. Spacecraft carry a supply of liquid oxygen on board as well as liquid fuel to enable their rockets to function in the airless environment of space.

Father of rocketry
A Russian schoolteacher named Konstantin Tsiolkovsky was the first person to develop written theories on rocket-powered space travel. He proposed the use of multi-stage rockets and liquid fuel. His ideas were first published in 1903.

Rocket weapon
A V-2 rocket blasts off during the 1940s. It was the world's first supersonic guided missile. The weapon was developed in Germany during the Second World War (1939-45). One of its designers, Wernher von Braun, joined the US space program after the war. He later headed the design team for the Saturn V rocket, which took astronauts to the Moon.

Liquid fuel rocket
American engineer Robert Goddard prepares to launch the world's first rocket propelled by a liquid fuel. Goddard's rocket was launched in 1926. Before this all rockets had been propelled by burning a solid fuel. Goddard's rocket soared to a height of 56m/184ft at a speed of almost 100kph/ 62 mph.

Second stage

Liquid oxygen tank

Payload

Liquid hydrogen fuel tank

Helium tank

Combustion chamber

Vulcain rocket engine

First stage

Solid rocket boosters

Inside Ariane 5

This illustration shows the inner workings of an Ariane 5 rocket, one of the largest launch vehicles of the European Space Agency's Ariane series. The Ariane rockets have launched many of the world's science and communications satellites. Ariane 5 is made of two rocket stages stacked on top of each other, with the payload housed in the nose cone. Two solid rocket boosters attached to the main body provide extra thrust. Each stage and both boosters are jettisoned (discarded) once they have used up their fuel. This reduces the weight of the rocket as it ascends.

Nose cone contains satellite payload

Ariane 5 launch sequence

Ready for launch

An Ariane 5 rocket stands on its launch-pad ready for lift-off. Its nose cone can hold up to three satellites, which it will launch into orbit around the earth. The most powerful Ariane 5 rockets can launch payloads weighing up to 21 tons.

Launch

Lift-off! The main stage of the Ariane 5 burns about 130 tons of liquid hydrogen and 26 tons of liquid oxygen. Each of the rocket boosters burn 237 tons of solid fuel as the Ariane 5 powers up through the atmosphere.

Booster separation

At a height of 55km/34 miles above the Earth, only 129 seconds after lift-off, the two solid rocket boosters have exhausted their fuel supply. The rocket boosters are then jettisoned from the main body of the Ariane 5 vehicle.

Launching a satellite

At a height of 110km/68 miles, the nose cone fairing of the Ariane 5 is jettisoned. The small second stage then carries the two satellites up into orbit. Finally, they are released into space.

ESCAPING FROM EARTH

Orbital insertion

Circular orbit

Elliptical orbit

Highly elliptical orbit

Escape

THE function of a rocket designed for spaceflight is to carry a satellite or astronauts into space. In order to do that, it has to overcome gravity (the force that pulls everything down to Earth). If the rocket's engines are not powerful enough, gravity will win and pull the rocket and its payload back to Earth. With more powerful engines, the rocket's attempt to fly away into space is exactly equalled by the pull of gravity. With these two forces in perfect balance, a spacecraft will continue to circle the Earth. If the rocket is more powerful, it can fly fast enough to escape from Earth's gravity altogether and fly away towards the Moon or the planets. The speed that it needs to reach to do this is called escape velocity. You can demonstrate the speeds needed for escape velocity by trying out a simple experiment using a magnet and ball-bearings. Then try launching your own cork model rocket from a plastic bottle.

Escape velocity

To go into orbit around the Earth, a spacecraft must reach a velocity of at least 28,500kph/17,700 mph. Depending on how fast it is travelling, the spacecraft may go into a circular, elliptical, or highly elliptical orbit. If it reaches a velocity of 40,200kph/25,000 mph, the spacecraft escapes from the Earth's gravity altogether.

LAUNCH A CHEMICAL ROCKET

You will need: baking soda, paper towel, water, vinegar, large plastic bottle, paper streamers, cork, drawing pin (push pin).

A chemical reaction between the vinegar (representing liquid oxygen) and baking soda (representing fuel) produces carbon dioxide gas. The gas pressure inside the bottle pushes against the cork. The cork is blasted into the air like a rocket lifting off.

3 Push the cork in immediately so that it is a snug fit, but not too tight. Quickly take the bottle outside. Then move at least 3m/10ft away from it and watch what happens.

1 Place a teaspoon of baking soda directly in the middle of a 10cm x 20cm/4 x 8in piece of paper towel. Roll up the towel and twist the ends to keep the baking soda fuel inside.

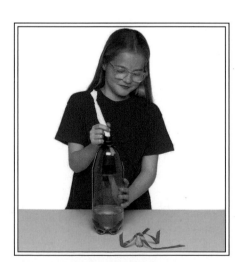

2 Pour half a cup of water and the same amount of vinegar into the bottle. Fix paper streamers to the top of the cork with a drawing pin. Drop the towel inside.

ESCAPING FROM GRAVITY

You will need: thin card, ruler, pencil, scissors, magnetic strip, 10cm x 5cm/4 x 2in piece of plastic, baking tray, modelling clay, sticky tape, small steel ball-bearings.

1 Measure out a 30cm x 10cm/12 x 4in strip of thin card using a ruler. Cut it out with the scissors. Fold it lengthways into three sections to form an M-shaped trough.

2 Cut the magnetic strip into 5 short pieces. Glue these short strips to the plastic base to make a large, square bar magnet, as shown above.

3 Fix the magnet firmly to one end of the tray with some of the modelling clay. Position it roughly in the middle. The magnet simulates the pull of the Earth's gravity.

4 Position one end of the trough over the edge of the magnet. Attach it to the magnet with sticky tape. The trough represents the path of a rocket as it ascends into orbit.

5 Roll the remaining modelling clay into a round ball. Position the clay ball underneath the other end of the M-shaped trough. This raises the trough at a slight angle.

6 Place a small ball bearing at the end of the trough and let it roll down. The ball-bearing sticks to the magnet. The velocity of the ball-bearing rocket along the trough's flight path is not fast enough to escape the pull of the magnet.

Ball-bearing escapes the pull of the magnet

7 Raise the trough and roll another ball-bearing along it. The steeper angle increases the ball-bearing's velocity. Keep raising the trough and rolling ball-bearings until one shoots past the magnet. It has then achieved escape velocity!

THE FIRST SPACE FLIGHTS

AFTER the Second World War (1939-45), the United States and the Soviet Union raced against each other to build a rocket powerful enough to reach space. On October 4, 1957, the world learned that the Soviet Union had won the race. It had successfully placed the first artificial satellite, *Sputnik 1*, in orbit. Getting a satellite of any sort into space successfully was an achievement because rocket launchers often failed. They frequently blew up or flew off course. As these early liquid fuel rockets were not very powerful, the first satellites had to be very small and simple. But soon, larger and more reliable rockets were built. They could launch bigger, heavier satellites. These satellites were designed to do different jobs. Weather satellites made weather forecasts more accurate, while science satellites carried out scientific research. Communications satellites relayed telephone calls and television shows around the world, and Earth resources satellites studied the planet. The Space Age had begun.

Artificial satellite
The first artificial satellite, *Sputnik 1*, was a metal sphere measuring 58cm/23in across and weighing 84kg/185lb. Its radio transmitter sent a signal down to Earth for 21 days. After 96 days the satellite re-entered the atmosphere and burned up.

V2 technology
A modified V2 blasts off from an American launch pad in 1950. V2 rockets captured in Germany during the Second World War were taken to America. They were used to develop rockets for the US space programme.

Chimp in space
Ham the chimpanzee was launched into space on January 31st 1961. His mission was to test the safety of the Mercury capsule, which would be used to carry the first American astronaut into space. Ham survived his flight, proving the capsule was safe for humans.

Sputnik 2 *capsule*

Instruments measured Laika's pulse, blood pressure and heartbeat

Animal testing
This model shows the dog Laika inside *Sputnik 2*. On November 3, 1957, the Soviet Union launched *Sputnik 2* into orbit with Laika on-board. She became the first living creature in space. *Sputnik 2* circled the world for a total of seven days. Its mission was to test the effects of spaceflight on an animal to see if it was safe to send a human into space. Unfortunately, Laika died a few hours after the launch due to overheating, possibly caused by a failure of the sustainer rocket to separate from the capsule.

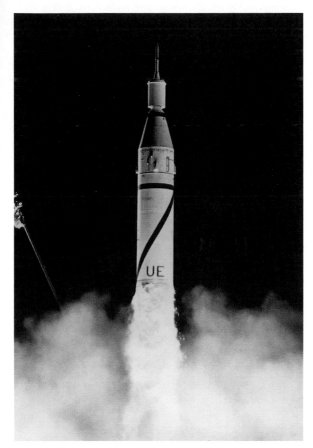

Weather satellites

A TIROS satellite sits on top of a launch vehicle as it is fuelled for lift-off. A total of 10 TIROS satellites were launched between 1960 and 1965. They were the first weather satellites. Each TIROS satellite took 16 photographs of the Earth on every orbit. The photographs were then transmitted to Earth by radio when a ground receiving station came within range. The name TIROS stands for Television and Infra-Red Observation Satellite.

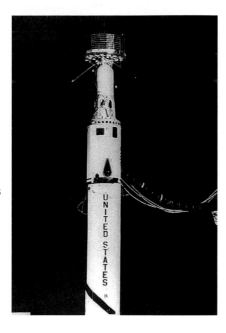

Explorer 1
The United States' first satellite, *Explorer 1*, clears the launch pad on January 31st 1958. The satellite's on-board instruments detected belts of intense radiation around the Earth. They were named the Van Allen belts, after the scientist who analysed the satellite's data.

Radio antenna

Solar panels

Photographs from space

The satellite *Explorer 6* was launched on August 7, 1959. It sent back the first photograph of the Earth taken from space. For the first time in the history of humanity, people were finally able to see their home planet as one world. More than 50 Explorer satellites were launched over the next 16 years, providing scientists with a great deal of valuable information about space and the Sun.

Early Bird
The first privately owned communications satellite, or comsat, was called *Early Bird*. The satellite was also known as *Intelsat 1*. The orbiting spacecraft could be used to relay up to a maximum of 240 telephone calls or one television channel. *Early Bird* revolutionized international communications as it provided a regular service for the transmission of television pictures across the Atlantic Ocean.

PEOPLE IN SPACE

THE human exploration of space began with Yuri Gagarin's historic flight in *Vostok 1* in 1961. The Soviet cosmonaut made one orbit of the Earth. The United States entered the space race soon afterwards with its Mercury space project. These early spaceflights proved that human beings could travel into space and return safely to Earth. After six Vostok flights and six Mercury flights, both nations moved on to the next stage of their space programs. Soviet Voshkod flights achieved the first three-person flight and the first space walk, by Alexei Leonov. The United States launched 10 flights of the two-person Gemini spacecraft. These missions tried out all the manoeuvres needed for a Moon landing. Gemini astronauts learned how to locate other spacecraft, move towards them and dock (link up) with them. They also stayed in space for long periods, with the *Gemini 7* flight in 1965 lasting for a record 14 days. By the end of the Project Gemini flights, the US was ready to send astronauts to the Moon.

Vostok 1
The *Vostok 1* space capsule was a 2.3m/8 ft-wide sphere. For most of its flight, the capsule was attached to an instrument cylinder and rocket engine. The engine slowed the capsule to begin its descent from orbit and re-entry into the atmosphere.

Space pioneers
On April 12, 1961, the Soviet pilot Yuri Gagarin became the first man to fly into space. Valentina Tereshkova became the first woman in space on June 16, 1963. Her flight in *Vostok 6* lasted 70 hours.

The Mercury Seven
The seven original Mercury astronauts show off their new silver spacesuits. Alan Shepard became the first American in space on May 5, 1961. His Mercury capsule was fired up into space and dropped back immediately to Earth without going into orbit. John Glenn became the first American to orbit the Earth nine months later. Glenn did not go into space again until his historic flight aboard the Space Shuttle in 1998.

Alan Shepard   *Virgil Grissom*   *Gordon Cooper*

Walter Schirra

Donald Slayton   *John Glenn*   *Scott Carpenter*

Friendship 7
John Glenn's Mercury capsule rises off the launch pad atop an Atlas rocket on February 20, 1962. The capsule, named *Friendship 7*, orbited the Earth for more than four hours, before splashing down in the sea.

Horizon scanners

Pitch and yaw jet

Pilot's seat

Heat shield

Antenna housing

Main parachute compartment

Attitude controller

Retro-rockets

Inside a Mercury capsule
The Mercury capsule was tiny. It measured 2.92m/9½ft from top to bottom and 1.89m/6ft across the heat shield. The astronaut is seated with his back to the shield. The capsule's narrow nose housed the parachutes that slowed its descent through the atmosphere before splashdown.

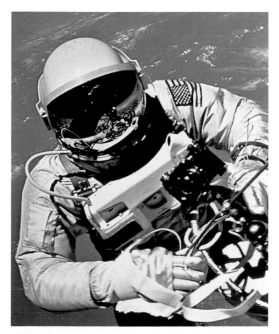

Walking in space
Ed White floats in space, connected to his space capsule by a thin tether. The 1965 *Gemini 4* flight saw White become the first US astronaut to perform a spacewalk.

Gemini splashdown
David Scott and Neil Armstrong breathe a sigh of relief in their *Gemini 8* capsule after splashdown. The 1966 mission almost ended in disaster. The astronauts only just regained control after a faulty thruster made the craft spin wildly. Armstrong later became the first person to walk on the Moon.

MOON MISSION

T HE 50 ton Apollo spacecraft needed the world's most powerful rocket, the Saturn V, to send it to the Moon and back. The Apollo spacecraft was made in three parts – the command module (CM), the service module (SM) and the lunar excursion module (LEM). The three-man crew lived in the tiny command module for the three-day flight to the Moon and for another three days on the return journey. The service module attached to it provided electricity and air to breathe. The lunar module was the strange, spider-like craft used to make the Moon landing. First, the Apollo spacecraft was checked out in Earth orbit by the *Apollo* 7 mission. In December 1968, *Apollo 8* travelled to the Moon, swung around behind it and returned to Earth. Two more practice missions followed. Then, in July 1969, *Apollo 11* made history by landing astronauts on the Moon for the first time.

The countdown begins
On May 25, 1961, the American President, John F. Kennedy, announced that the United States would land a man on the Moon by the end of the 1960s. It was a very ambitious plan, as the US had not yet sent an astronaut into orbit.

Apollo 11 **crew**
Neil Armstrong, Michael Collins and Edwin (Buzz) Aldrin were selected to be the first Apollo crew to land on the Moon. Armstrong was chosen as mission commander, in overall control of the spacecraft and crew. Aldrin had the job of flying the lunar excursion module (LEM). Collins was the command/service module (CSM) pilot, and remained in orbit while Armstrong and Aldrin walked on the surface of the Moon.

Command module (CM)

Service module (SM)

Lunar excursion module (LEM)

Instrument unit

Third stage

Third stage engine

Second stage engines

Second stage

First stage

First stage engines

Stabilizing fins

The Saturn V
This model shows the various components of the Saturn V launch vehicle. Its three rocket stages were jettisoned in turn as they used up their fuel. Only the third stage and the Apollo spacecraft modules reached the Moon.

Michael Collins

Neil Armstrong

Edwin (Buzz) Aldrin

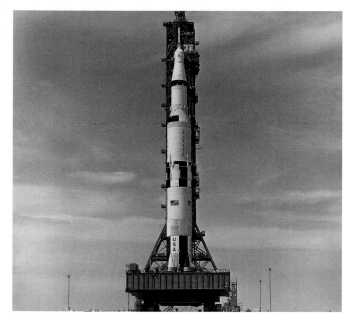

Crawler transporter

The Saturn V rocket and Apollo spacecraft roll slowly from the assembly building to the launch pad on top of a crawler transporter. This strange vehicle weighed 3,000 tons and needed a crew of 15 to operate it.

Lift-off!

The *Apollo 11* mission gets underway as the mighty Saturn V rises off the launch pad. The escape tower on the top of the rocket was jettisoned once the Saturn V was safely in flight. The enormous power of its five first-stage engines made the ground beneath the Saturn V shake like an earthquake. The rocket was driven upwards by the rush of hot exhaust gases from the engines. Exhaust from four of the first-stage engines balanced the weight of the 3,000 ton rocket as the fifth engine provided the thrust required for lift-off.

Approaching the Moon

The *Apollo 11* lunar module, called the *Eagle*, drops out of lunar orbit and heads for its landing site. The date is July 20, 1969. Inside it are Neil Armstrong and Buzz Aldrin. Shortly after touchdown, Neil Armstrong descends the lunar module ladder. As he places his foot on the lunar soil he says "That's one small step for a man – one giant leap for mankind."

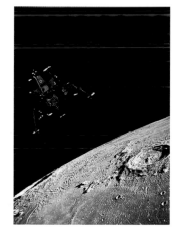

FACT BOX

• The distance between the Earth and the Moon is about 384,400km/238,855 miles.

• During the lunar day the Moon's surface temperature can be as high as 120°C/248°F. During the night, the temperature can drop as low as –144°C/-227.2°F.

• The Moon completes one full orbit of the Earth every 27 days and 8 hours.

Stepping out

Buzz Aldrin descends the *Eagle*'s ladder, becoming the second astronaut to walk on the Moon. His spacesuit's Portable Life Support System (PLSS) backpack is clearly visible as he lowers himself down. As he looks around at the Moon's lifeless surface, Aldrin describes the view as "magnificent desolation".

GOING TO THE MOON

PLOTTING a course to the Moon is not as easy as moving from place to place on a planet's surface. On Earth, people can navigate by following landmarks or natural features, such as hills, valleys and rivers. Pilots who fly at high altitudes navigate by using radio beacons on the ground or signals from satellites. The problem with travelling from the Earth to the Moon is that both of them are moving. If you set off from the Earth with your spacecraft aimed directly at the Moon, it will not be there by the time you arrive. The Moon will have moved on around its orbit. If you aim at the Moon and continually change your direction to follow its movements, you will use an enormous amount of fuel. The answer is to aim your spacecraft at the place where the Moon will be by the time you get there. However, you also need to make sure you are not drifting off course on the way. Spacecraft use one of the oldest navigation methods. They navigate by the stars. Try your hand at aiming at a moving target by following this simple project. You can also demonstrate staging by making your own two-stage rocket.

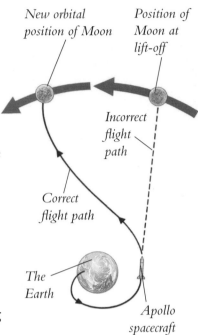

New orbital position of Moon   *Position of Moon at lift-off*

Incorrect flight path

Correct flight path

The Earth

Apollo spacecraft

Moving targets
This diagram shows two possible flight paths for an Apollo spacecraft. Aiming directly at the Moon does not take into account its movement as it orbits the Earth. The correct, efficient route compensates for the Moon's orbital movement by aiming ahead of its position at lift-off.

AIMING AT THE MOON

You will need: string, ruler, scissors, masking tape, metal washer, book, small balls of screwed-up paper.

1 Measure out 60cm/24in of string with the ruler. Cut it off with scissors. Tape one end of the string to one end of the ruler. Tie a washer to the other end of the string.

2 Place the ruler on a table or box with the string hanging over the edge. Weigh it down with a heavy book. Try hitting the washer by throwing small balls of paper at it.

3 Start the washer swinging and try to hit it again with the paper balls. See how much more difficult it is to hit a moving target, like a spacecraft aiming at a moving moon.

MAKE A TWO-STAGE ROCKET

1 Using scissors, carefully cut the bottom out of a paper or plastic cup. This will serve as the linking collar between the two stages of the balloon rocket.

2 Partly blow up the long balloon with the balloon pump. Pull its neck through the paper cup. This balloon will be your two-stage rocket's second stage.

3 Fold the neck of the long balloon over the side of the cup. Tape the end of the balloon's neck to the cup to stop the air from escaping, as shown.

You will need: 2 paper or plastic cups, scissors, long balloon, balloon pump, sticky tape, round balloon.

Second stage fires

First stage jettisoned

Second stage jettisoned

Third stage fires

Third stage powers command/service module (CSM) towards the Moon

Rocket staging

The Saturn V rocket had three stages. The first two powered the spacecraft up through the atmosphere. The third stage propelled it into orbit and then gave an extra push to send the craft on its way to the Moon.

4 Carefully push the round balloon into the open end of the paper or plastic cup. This balloon will form the first stage of your two-stage balloon rocket.

5 Blow up the round balloon so that it wedges the neck of the long balloon in place inside the cup. Hold the neck of the round balloon to keep the air inside it.

6 Peel the tape off the neck of the long balloon. Hold the rocket as shown. Let go of the round balloon's neck. Air rushes out, launching the first stage of the rocket. It then falls away, launching the second stage balloon.

EXPLORING THE MOON

APOLLO astronauts explored the Moon in two ways. On the earlier missions they walked on the surface in the area around the lunar module. On later trips, they also drove around in the lunar roving vehicle (LRV). They collected rock samples and laid out scientific instruments on the lunar surface. The instruments continued to send information about the Moon back to scientists on Earth after the astronauts left. To return to Earth, the upper part of the lunar module blasted off, using the base as a launch pad. It then docked with the command/service module (CSM). With all three astronauts on board the CSM again, the lunar module was jettisoned. The service module's rocket engine fired and set the CSM on course for the Earth. The command module separated from the service module for re-entry. Inside the atmosphere, parachutes slowed the capsule's descent before splashdown in the Pacific Ocean.

Man on the Moon
This famous photograph of Buzz Aldrin was taken by Neil Armstrong. If you look very closely, you can just see Armstrong and the lunar module reflected in Aldrin's helmet visor.

Footprints in the dust
The Apollo astronauts left behind many footprints and impressions in the lunar dust. They will still be there millions of years from now. Unlike the Earth, there is no wind on the Moon to disturb the footprints or rain to wash them away.

Jumping on the Moon
The Moon's pull of gravity is one-sixth of that of the Earth. This means you could jump six times farther and higher on the Moon than on Earth. You can demonstrate this by trying out a simple experiment. Lay a string in a straight line on the ground. Stand on one side of the string with your toes touching it. Jump as far as you can over the string. Ask someone to measure the distance from the string to where you landed. Multiply this by six to find out how far you could jump on the Moon.

Experiments on the moon
Apollo 12 astronaut Alan Bean sets up special instruments to detect moonquakes, measure the Moon's magnetic field and study solar wind particles. Each Apollo mission carried out a variety of different scientific experiments.

FACT BOX

• The Moon's gravitational pull on the Earth is the main cause of the regular rise and fall of the tides in our planet's many oceans and seas.

Apollo 13

Fred Haise, Jack Swigert and James Lovell were the crew members of the *Apollo 13* mission in 1971. An explosion inside the spacecraft's service module 330,000km/205,000 miles from Earth left the crew marooned in space. Tens of thousands of technicians on Earth worked round the clock to help the crew bring their damaged spacecraft safely home.

Lunar rover

Apollo 17 astronaut Eugene Cernan takes the lunar roving vehicle for a drive in the Taurus-Littrow region of the Moon. This small electric car was carried on the final three Apollo Moon missions (*Apollo 15, 16* and *17*). The vehicle enabled astronauts to travel further and collect more rock samples from a wider area.

Splashdown

Second stage jettisoned

Third stage/CSM

CSM docks with LEM

Upper part of LEM redocks with CSM

CM re-enters the Earth's atmosphere

CM separates from SM

CSM heads back for Earth

CSM/LEM enters lunar orbit

LEM undocks from CSM to land on the Moon

An Apollo mission

This illustration shows the various stages of an Apollo Moon mission. One of the most dangerous stages was re-entry into the Earth's atmosphere. The command module had to hit the atmosphere at exactly the right angle. Too shallow an angle would cause the spacecraft to bounce back into space. Too steep an angle would cause it to burn up in the Earth's atmosphere.

Splashdown
The *Apollo 17* command module splashes down in the Pacific Ocean. After a high speed re-entry into the atmosphere, the capsule floats slowly down under three huge parachutes. Splashdown marked the end of an Apollo mission. Recovery crews waiting in nearby ships rushed to the spacecraft to help the astronauts out of the capsule.

LIVING IN SPACE

THE human body evolved over millions of years to live on the surface of the Earth. It is totally unsuited to living in space, where there is no air, little gravity and it is freezing cold in the shade and roasting hot in direct sunshine. Astronauts have to take Earth-like conditions with them into space. They need air to breathe, warmth, food, water and light. They also require radio equipment to keep in touch with each other and with mission controllers on Earth. Life support systems and communications equipment all need electricity, so they have to take an electricity generator with them too. The human body is very good at changing to suit the conditions around it. During long space missions, these changes can become a problem. Without gravity to work against, muscles waste away and bones lose calcium. To stay healthy, astronauts exercise using special machines.

Controlling moisture
Place a lamp by a glass jar so its heat makes water at the bottom of the jar evaporate. The jar's cooler sides cause the vapour to condense back into water. Heat from the Sun makes this happen inside a spacesuit too, but the suit's systems remove the moisture.

Life in the ISS
Crew-members aboard the International Space Station (ISS) carry out scientific research in biology, physics, astronomy and other fields. Their work includes studying the effects of long spaceflights on the human body.

Space toilet
Going to the toilet in space is difficult because of the weightless conditions. Everything floats! A special toilet is installed in the International Space Station. A brisk stream of air makes sure that everything goes in the right direction!

Space meals
Astronauts eat a tasty menu chosen by them from a selection of fresh food and food preserved by heat or radiation. It is packed in tins, foil pouches and clear plastic.

Keeping fit
Daily exercise is essential for staying healthy during a long spaceflight. Each astronaut on the International Space Station spends up to two hours a day exercising on a variety of machines. Sometimes, they have to use elastic ropes called bungee cords to stop them from floating away while exercising. The cords also provide some resistance for the astronauts to work against to stop their muscles wasting away.

Sleeping while weightless

Most space station astronauts sleep inside zip-up bags called sleep restraints. Some sleep inside individual compartments. Others sleep outside these units. They fasten their sleep restraint to the floor, a wall or the ceiling to stop them from floating about. One astronaut, Marc Garneau, preferred to sleep floating free.

Dressing for space

An International Space Station astronaut prepares for her Extra-Vehicular Activity (EVA), or spacewalk. First she puts on a liquid-cooling and ventilation garment. Cool water pumped through a network of tubing stops the astronaut from overheating in space. Next, she steps into the spacesuit legs and lower body. Then she wriggles up inside the suit's upper body and locks the two suit halves together. The astronaut then puts on a radio headset. Finally, the helmet and gloves are locked into place.

Tubes carrying water around garment

Lower half of spacesuit

Liquid-cooling and ventilation garment

Upper half of space suit

Locking ring

Lower half of space suit

Helmet

Radio headset

Gloves

Extra-Vehicular Activity

Astronauts sometimes have to work outside their spacecraft. This is called Extra-Vehicular Activity (EVA). An EVA is also known as a spacewalk. International Space Station astronauts have made more than 300 spacewalks to build the station and carry out repair and maintenance work on it. They wear spacesuits with life-support backpacks that enable them to survive in the harsh environment of space. The backpack supplies oxygen to breathe and keeps the astronaut at a comfortable temperature.

FACT BOX

• On early spaceflights, spacesuits were made specially for each astronaut. Astronauts now wear off-the-peg spacesuits that are made in a range of sizes.

• Russian cosmonaut Valeriy Poliyakov holds the record for the longest continuous period of time spent in space. He stayed on board the *Mir* space station for a total of 437 consecutive days.

SPACE SHUTTLE

Shuttle transporter
The Space Shuttle was carried on the same crawler transporter that moved Saturn V rockets from the assembly building to the launch pad. Each Shuttle made this journey many times during its working life.

For the first 24 years of the Space Age, every rocket and spacecraft was specially designed for one mission only. Nothing was used for a second time. This was an extremely costly and wasteful method of going into space. Scientists realised that if spaceflight was ever to become as commonplace as other ways to travel, spacecraft must be re-usable, like aircraft or ships. The world's first re-usable spacecraft, the United States' Space Shuttle, was launched for the first time on April 12, 1981. The Space Shuttle Orbiter was a space plane. It was about the same size as a small airliner. The spacecraft was designed to take off like a rocket, complete its mission in space, return to Earth and land on a runway like an aircraft. Its short, stubby wings helped it to glide down through the atmosphere. The US Orbiter also had a large payload bay. It was used for carrying satellites or other structures into space, or for bringing them back to Earth for repair. The Space Shuttle made its last flight in 2011.

Orbital manoeuvring engines — Payload bay — Cockpit — Nose thrusters — Main engines — Tail thrusters — External fuel tank (ET) — Solid rocket boosters (SRBs)

Shuttle launch
With its two solid rocket boosters and three main engines firing, the Space Shuttle rises off the pad. It accelerates rapidly into the sky.

Space Shuttle stack
The Space Shuttle stack consisted of the Orbiter, an external fuel tank (ET) and two solid rocket boosters (SRBs). The Orbiter was attached to the giant external fuel tank, which supplied its three main engines with liquid hydrogen fuel and liquid oxygen during the launch. The SRBs were attached to either side of the ET to provide extra take-off power. In space, smaller orbital manoeuvring engines took over. Even smaller thrusters in the nose and tail were used to make adjustments to the Orbiter's position.

Shuttle cockpit
The Space Shuttle being flown by the mission commander and pilot, who sit on the flight deck in the Orbiter's nose. They are surrounded by control panels and computer screens.

Lifting bodies

The HL-10 aircraft *(below)* is a lifting body, one of a series of test vehicles built before the Orbiter was designed. Lifting bodies were designed to test how a vehicle with very short wings would fly. This shape was chosen as it would survive the heat of re-entry and could also be flown like a plane inside the atmosphere.

The X-15

During the 1960s, long before the Space Shuttle was built, another rocket plane was flying to the fringes of the atmosphere. The X-15 was an experimental plane used to study flight at very great heights. Results from the X-15 test flights were used to help design and develop the Space Shuttle.

Shuttle mission profile

Two minutes after launch, at a height of 45km/28 miles, the solid rocket boosters fall away. Six minutes later, the main engines shut down and the external tank is jettisoned. The orbital manoeuvring engines then fire twice to insert the Orbiter in orbit about 400km/250 miles above the Earth. When the mission is completed, the Orbiter manoeuvres for re-entry. It fires its orbital engines to slow it down (retro-fire), and then begin its descent. After re-entry, the Shuttle glides to a landing, usually touching down at the Kennedy Space Centre in Florida, USA.

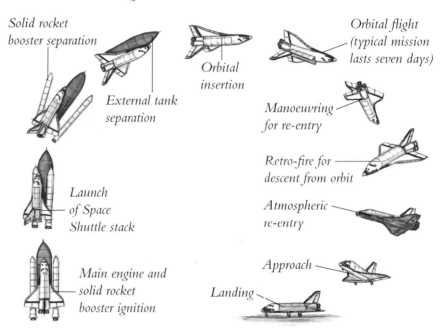

Solid rocket booster separation

External tank separation

Orbital insertion

Orbital flight (typical mission lasts seven days)

Manoeuvring for re-entry

Retro-fire for descent from orbit

Atmospheric re-entry

Launch of Space Shuttle stack

Main engine and solid rocket booster ignition

Approach

Landing

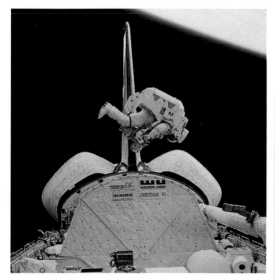

Human spacecraft

Astronaut Bruce McCandless floats above the payload bay. He is wearing the manned manoeuvring unit (MMU), a gas-powered jetpack that allows him to manoeuvre in space independently from the Shuttle.

Soviet shuttle

This is the *Buran* shuttle built by the Soviet Union during the 1980s. Like the US Orbiter, *Buran* was protected from the searing heat of re-entry by glassy silica tiles and fire-proof cloth. The Soviet shuttle was only launched into space once, completing two orbits of the Earth in November 1988. *Buran* did not carry a crew on its flight and returned to Earth under automatic control.

WORKING IN SPACE

Working in a spacesuit
Bulky spacesuits make working in space difficult. Spacesuit designers are always trying to improve them. The more flexible a suit is, the less tiring it is to work in. This in turn enables an astronaut to work outside for longer periods.

Working inside an orbiting spacecraft is a little more difficult than working on Earth, because astronauts in space are weightless. On Earth, gravity pulls us down and also gives us something to push against. If a weightless astronaut pushes a handle in zero-gravity, the astronaut flies away in the opposite direction! So astronauts have to be anchored to something solid before they can do any work. Outside a spacecraft, a spacesuit makes it even more difficult to work. The astronaut has to work against the suit to close a hand or bend an arm or leg. Spacesuit gloves have thin rubber fingerpads so that astronauts can feel things through them, but they are still hard to work with. Simulate working in space by following an experiment using rubber gloves, a bowl of water and some nuts and bolts. Then try making a robot arm like the International Space Station's remote manipulator system (RMS), which is used by its crew to launch and retrieve satellites.

WORKING IN ZERO-GRAVITY

You will need: nuts and bolts, rubber gloves, bowl, water.

1 Take the nuts and bolts and place them on a table. Now try picking them up and screwing them together. You should find this a very easy task to achieve!

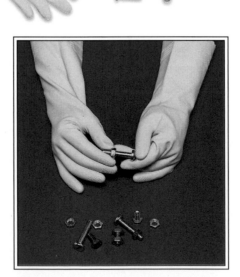

2 Now try screwing the nuts and bolts together with the gloves on. This is more difficult, like trying to carry out a delicate task on Earth wearing bulky spacesuit gloves.

3 Fill the bowl with water. Add the nuts and bolts. Try screwing them together with the gloves on. This is very difficult, like working in a spacesuit outside a spacecraft.

MAKE A ROBOT ARM

1 Use the ruler to measure out three 28cm x 5cm/11in x 2in card strips. Cut them out. Make a 2.5cm/1in hole from the end of each strip. Join the strips with split pins, as shown.

2 Take the hook and screw it into the end of the dowel. The dowel will be used to remotely control the robot arm, just like real astronauts remotely operate the RMS.

3 Now carefully bend one of the paperclips into the shape of the letter S. To attach the paperclip, pass it through the hole in the end of the cardboard arm, as shown.

You will need: thick cardboard, ruler, scissors, bradawl (hole punch), 2 split pins (paper fasteners), dowel, picture hook, 2 paper clips, ball of modelling clay.

Remote manipulator system
The International Space Station's robot arm is controlled by an astronaut inside the space station. It was used to help build the station and now moves parts and supplies around the station.

5 Pass the hook on the dowel through the hole in the end of the cardboard arm. Move the dowel to remotely operate the robot arm. Try to pick up the ball using the S-shaped paper clip.

4 Take the modelling clay and roll it into a ball about the size of a walnut. Then take the second paperclip and push it firmly into the clay ball, as shown.

SPACE STATIONS

A SPACE STATION IS a spacecraft that stays in orbit for the whole of its working life. A crew live and work on board the station. The first, smallest space stations were launched into space in one piece. Later, larger stations were launched in pieces and put together in orbit. Space stations enable astronauts to carry out experiments lasting months or even years, and to make observations of the Sun and the Earth over long periods. The first space station was the Soviet Union's *Salyut 1*, launched in 1971. It was the first of a series of Salyut stations, which ended with *Salyut 7*, launched in April 1982. The first American space station was *Skylab*, which was put into space in May 1973. Although it suffered serious damage during launch, the station was visited by three crews who lived and worked on board until February 1974. In 1986, the Soviet Union launched a space station called *Mir*. When extra parts were added, it became the biggest spacecraft ever built. *Mir* was overtaken by the even bigger International Space Station (ISS). The first part of the ISS was launched in 1998.

Refrigeration system radiator

Living quarters

Orbital workshop

Telescope solar panel

Apollo telescope mount

Apollo command/service module (CSM)

Main solar panel

Equipment storage

Multiple docking adaptor

Skylab
The launch of the *Skylab* space station almost ended in disaster. One of its main solar panels and a heat shield were torn off by violent shaking during the launch. The first crew that visited it had to carry out emergency repairs. *Skylab* allowed scientists to analyze and study the Earth's surface and its atmosphere from space. A *Skylab* crew consisted of three people. Three crews lived lived aboard the station for 28, 59 and 84 days respectively.

Salyut 7

The main body of *Salyut 7* was 13m/42ft long by 4.2m/13ft across and weighed 19 tons. The station had three main parts – a docking port for spacecraft to link up with it, a mid-section (equipped with a laboratory and living quarters) and a propulsion module.

Mir

The space station *Mir* provided important information on the long-term effects of living in space. This will prove useful for future long-distance space missions, some of which may last for several years. The ageing Russian station suffered many breakdowns. Overcoming them also provided valuable experience in operating spacecraft for long periods of time.

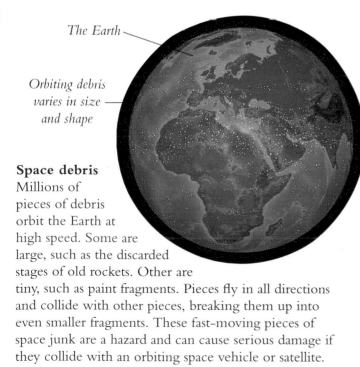

The Earth

Orbiting debris varies in size and shape

Space debris

Millions of pieces of debris orbit the Earth at high speed. Some are large, such as the discarded stages of old rockets. Other are tiny, such as paint fragments. Pieces fly in all directions and collide with other pieces, breaking them up into even smaller fragments. These fast-moving pieces of space junk are a hazard and can cause serious damage if they collide with an orbiting space vehicle or satellite.

International Space Station

The International Space Station (ISS) was built by 16 countries, including the USA, Russia, Japan, Canada and many European nations. It orbits Earth 16 times a day at a speed of 27,700kph/17,200mph. It is big enough to be seen with the naked eye if you know where to look.

ARTIFICIAL GRAVITY

Wheels in space
The film *2001: A Space Odyssey* featured a fictional rotating wheel-shaped space station. In theory, the centrifugal force generated by its rotation would create artificial gravity, holding people and objects against the walls of the wheel.

Space astronauts in orbit or far away from Earth do not feel the pull of gravity. They feel weightless, as if they are forever falling. In a state of weightlessness there is no up or down, because up and down are created by gravity. Even experienced pilots and astronauts sometimes feel uncomfortable or ill until they get used to being weightless. Weightlessness also has damaging effects on the human body. Future space stations and spacecraft designed for very long spaceflights may create artificial gravity to protect their occupants from the effects of weightlessness. One theoretical method of creating artificial gravity is to use rotation. Moving objects tend to travel in straight lines. When you whirl around a ball attached to the end of a piece of string, it tries to fly off in a straight line, stopped only by the string. Inside a rotating spacecraft, the solid outer walls would stop astronauts flying off in straight lines. The centrifugal force generated by the rotation would hold them against the outside walls, just as the Earth's gravity keeps us on the ground.

MAKE A CENTRIFUGE

You will need: 4 thick card triangles (30cm x 10cm x 22.5cm / 12in x 4in x 9in), plastic bottle, sticky tape, bradawl (hole punch), wooden skewer), long rubber band, masking tape, 3 paper clips, pliers, thick card strip (50cm x 5cm / 20in x 2in), small bead, drinking straw, 2 small plastic cups, modelling clay, water, food colouring.

1 Take the 4 card triangles and tape them to the sides of the bottle, as shown. These will provide the plastic bottle centrifuge with a broad, stable base to stand on.

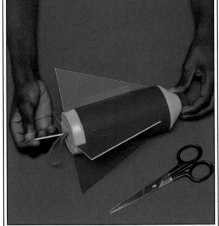

2 Using the bradawl, make a hole in the bottom of the plastic bottle. Push one end of the rubber band nearly all the way into the hole using a short wooden skewer.

3 Pass the wooden skewer right through the small loop of rubber band projecting from the hole, as shown. Leave an equal amount of stick on either side of the bottle.

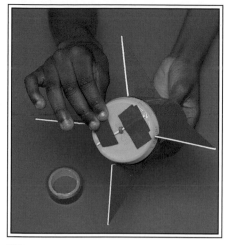

4 Take the masking tape and firmly secure the wooden skewer to the base of the plastic bottle. Make sure that the skewer is fixed so tightly that it cannot move.

5 Straighten out one end of a paper clip with pliers. Dip the hooked end of the clip into the neck of the bottle. Catch the rubber band with the hook and pull it out.

6 Using the scissors, make a hole in the middle of the 50cm x 5cm/20in x 2in strip. Thread the end of the paper clip through the bead then through the hole in the card.

7 Carefully bend the end of the paper clip down on to the cardboard strip. Using sticky tape, fix the end of the clip securely into place, as shown.

8 Use the scissors to cut two short pieces of drinking straw. Each piece should measure 5cm/2in in length. Fix one piece to each end of the cardboard strip with sticky tape.

9 Take one of the small plastic cups. Make a hole with the scissors on either side of the cup near the top. Now make holes in the second cup in the same way.

10 Straighten two paper clips with pliers. Thread a clip through each of the straws. Use the pliers to bend the ends of the clips down into hooks. Attach the cups by threading the ends of the clips through the holes, as shown. Make sure the cups can swing freely.

11 Stick the centrifuge to a flat surface with modelling clay. Fill the cups one-quarter full with water. Add food colouring to make the water show up clearly. Then turn the card strip until the rubber band is wound up. Let the strip go and watch the cups as it spins around rapidly. The cups fly outwards, but the water is held in place by centrifugal force.

ROBOT EXPLORERS

Most of the Solar System's planets are too far away from us to send astronauts to explore them. Instead, robot explorers are sent to be our eyes and ears in the distant reaches of the Solar System. They have either landed on or flown past every planet in the Solar System. On their travels, they have taken close-up photographs of the planets and their moons and taken measurements from their surfaces and atmospheres. *Luna 1* was the first space probe, heading out towards the Moon in 1959. *Mariner* spacecraft then flew by Mercury, Venus and Mars. The *Venera* probes landed on the surface of Venus and the *Viking* landers touched down on Mars. The most widely journeyed deep space probes are *Pioneer 10* and *11*, and *Voyager 1* and *2*, which have toured the Solar System's outer planets. They used the pull of gravity from each planet they passed to change their course and speed them on their way to the next planet.

A message from Earth
Pioneer 10 and *11* carried a message from Earth. Inscriptions on a metal plate fixed to the each of the probes showed a man and a woman, and the location in space of the Earth and the Sun.

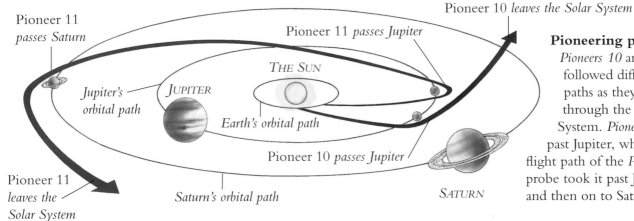

Pioneer 11 *passes Saturn*

Pioneer 11 *passes Jupiter*

Pioneer 10 *leaves the Solar System*

THE SUN

JUPITER

Jupiter's orbital path

Earth's orbital path

Pioneer 10 *passes Jupiter*

Pioneer 11 *leaves the Solar System*

Saturn's orbital path

SATURN

Pioneering probes
Pioneers 10 and *11* followed different flight paths as they travelled through the Solar System. *Pioneer 10* flew past Jupiter, while the flight path of the *Pioneer 11* probe took it past Jupiter and then on to Saturn.

Volcanic activity on Venus
This radar image was taken by the *Magellan* probe in orbit around the planet Venus. It shows Ushas Mons, a volcano in the southern hemisphere that rises 2km/1¼ miles above the planet's surface. Lava flows stretch for hundreds of miles away from the volcano.

Neptune fly-by
Voyager 2 flew past the distant planet Neptune in 1989. The images sent back by the probe reveal a strange, inhospitable world. The surface is completely hidden from view by a blue haze of methane gas, and high, wispy white clouds made from frozen methane.

Mars Rover

Four electric vehicles called
rovers have been sent to Mars.
The tiny *Sojourner* vehicle
was the first, in 1997. Two
larger rovers called *Spirit* and
Opportunity landed in 2004.
They were expected to work
for 90 days, but *Spirit* worked
until 2010 and *Opportunity*
was still working in 2014.
The biggest Mars rover, a
nuclear-powered vehicle
called *Curiosity* (*right*), landed
in 2012. The rovers
discovered that Mars once
had water on its surface.

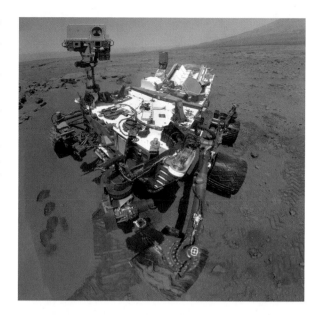

Galileo mission

As the *Galileo* spacecraft
approached Jupiter in
1995, it sent a probe into
the gas giant's atmosphere.
As the probe descended
into the clouds, it began
sending back information
to the orbiter. The orbiter
in turn relayed the data
back to receivers on Earth.
The *Galileo* probe
continued to transmit
its data about
Jupiter for 57
minutes. It was then
destroyed by heat and
the intense atmospheric
pressure of the gas giant.

Galileo
orbiter

Galileo *probe
separates from
orbiter*

Magellan probe

The *Magellan*
space probe went
into orbit around
Venus in 1990.
Its mission was to
map the planet's
surface. Radar was
used to reveal the
surface features, as
radio signals can
pass through the
thick clouds that
hide the planet's
surface from view.

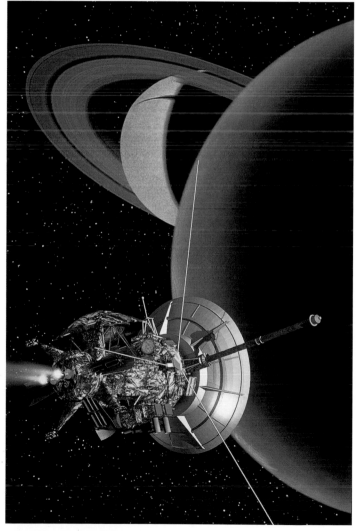

Mission to Saturn

The *Cassini-Huygens* spacecraft has been orbiting Saturn
since 2004. One part, a mini-probe called *Huygens*, landed
on Saturn's biggest moon, Titan. The main spacecraft,
Cassini, went on to explore Saturn and its other moons.

SLINGSHOTS AND ANTENNAE

GALILEO, *Cassini-Huygens* and many other space probes used gravity boosts to help them travel through the solar system. To get a boost, a probe passes by a planet and becomes attracted by its gravity. It is then pulled along by the planet on its orbit around the sun. Some of the planet's orbital speed is transferred to the probe, which is then catapulted towards the next planet to be visited. This slingshot effect is vital, as robot spacecraft could not carry enough fuel to change course from planet to planet. You can see how the slingshot effect works by trying this simple project using a magnet and a steel ball. The second project shows why many of the radio antennae used on the ground and on spacecraft are dish-shaped. The bowl shape of the antenna enables it to collect waves of radio energy. Its curve reflects the waves and brings them together at one point, concentrating all of the collected radio energy.

Slingshot around Jupiter
The space probe *Voyager 2* used several gravity assists to travel around the solar system. To get to Saturn, the probe received a gravity boost from Jupiter. The shells around Jupiter in this artist's visualization represent the gas giant's gravitational field. When *Voyager 2* reached Saturn, it used the slingshot effect again to re-direct itself towards Uranus.

GRAVITY BOOST

You will need: 2 thick books (of equal thickness), 60cm x 30cm/24in x 12in piece of thick cardboard, marble-sized steel ball, strong magnet, 30cm/12in wooden dowels (x2), sticky tape.

1 Place the books flat on a table 15cm/6in apart. Lay the piece of cardboard on top of the book, then roll the steel-ball space probe across it. It moves smoothly across the surface.

2 Place the magnet under the cardboard. Roll the steel-ball probe across the card. It is drawn towards the magnet planet by the gravity-like pull of its magnetic field.

3 Tape the magnet to the dowels. Roll the ball and then pull the magnet away. The ball speeds up and is pulled along by the magnet planet, like a probe getting a gravity boost.

MAKE A DISH ANTENNA

1 Draw 9 thin slits on the postcard using the pencil and ruler. Each slit should measure 2.5cm x 0.5cm/1in x ¹/₅in. They should be spaced from each other 0.5cm/¹/₅in apart.

2 Using the scissors, carefully cut out the slits in the postcard. The slits in the card will filter light, splitting it up into thin rays that will reflect off the curve of the antenna.

3 Place the large piece of thick cardboard on a table. Stand the postcard 40cm/16in from one end of the card, with the slits facing down. Fix it in position with clay.

You will need: plain postcard, pencil, ruler, scissors, 60cm x 100cm/23¹/₂in x 39in piece of thick cardboard, modelling clay, 20cm x 50cm/8in x 20in strip of mirror or metallic board, torch (flashlight).

Beaming waves
Dish antennae reflect their collected radio energy onto the receiver. Space probes use their antennae to receive radio signals from mission control on Earth. The receiver can also act as a transmitter, enabling the probe to send back its findings to Earth.

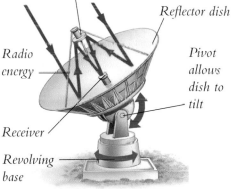

Secondary mirror reflects radio energy onto receiver

Reflector dish

Radio energy

Pivot allows dish to tilt

Receiver

Revolving base

4 Bend the reflective metallic board to form a semi-circular antenna, as shown. Stand it at one end of the thick cardboard base. Then fix it firmly in position using modelling clay.

5 Switch on the flashlight. Direct the light beam so that it shines through the slits in the postcard. The light is split into thin rays, which reflect off the metallic board.

6 Darken the room. Move the flashlight until the light rays reflecting off the curved mirror are brought together at one spot, like radio waves on a dish antenna.

SPACE COMMUNICATIONS

Everyone's lives are affected by modern space technology. Communications satellites (comsats) relay telephone calls around the world and beam television shows directly into our homes. Meteorological satellites provide highly accurate weather forecasts and navigation satellites tell crews of ships and aircraft exactly where they are. Earth resources satellites study the Earth's oceans, forests and rocks and radio their findings down from space. Collecting information at a distance like this is called remote sensing. Astronomers know infinitely more about the Solar System because of information sent back from probes. They also use space technology to look for radio signals produced by intelligent beings elsewhere in the Universe.

Comsat

A communications satellite needs antennae to receive and re-transmit radio signals. It also needs electricity to power its radio equipment. The comsat's solar cells convert sunlight directly into electricity.

Solar cells

Telstar

On 10 July 1962, the Telstar comsat was launched. It was able to receive messages from the ground, amplify them, and then immediately re-transmit them. This made it possible to beam live television broadcasts across the Atlantic Ocean for the first time.

Omni-directional (all direction) radio antenna

Dish-shaped radio antenna

Satellite navigation

A geologist checks his position using a hand-held Global Positioning System (GPS) receiver. The GPS is a network of 32 satellites in orbit around the Earth. Radio signals are sent out by the satellites, marking their position in orbit. The receiver picks up signals from at least three of the satellites. This enables the user to pinpoint the receiver's position to within 15m/49ft.

FACT BOX

• Radio signals sent from Earth to a satellite are called the uplink. Signals sent from a satellite to Earth are called the downlink.

• The first comsat, *Echo 1*, was launched in 1960. The inflatable 33m/108ft-wide comsat resembled a balloon. It was used to reflect radio signals.

Envisat

Satellites monitor Earth's climate and environment. A European satellite called Envisat spent ten years studying Earth after its launch by an Ariane 5 rocket in 2002. Its ten instruments studied the atmosphere, ocean waves, farming, shipping, floods, snow and ice.

Communications dishes

Radio signals are sent to and received from satellites by using large dish antennae. The size of the dish enables it to collect as much energy as possible from the low-power transmitters used by most satellites. Some satellites move across the sky, so the dish has to be able to tilt and turn to follow them.

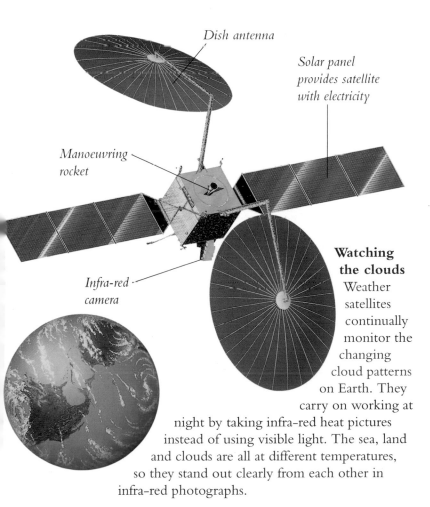

Dish antenna

Solar panel provides satellite with electricity

Manoeuvring rocket

Infra-red camera

Watching the clouds

Weather satellites continually monitor the changing cloud patterns on Earth. They carry on working at night by taking infra-red heat pictures instead of using visible light. The sea, land and clouds are all at different temperatures, so they stand out clearly from each other in infra-red photographs.

Monitoring the Earth

This picture of North-eastern America was taken by a remote sensing satellite. The images produced by these satellites help to make maps, monitor pollution and study the geology of an area. They are also used to monitor rainforest destruction.

RELAYING RADIO WAVES

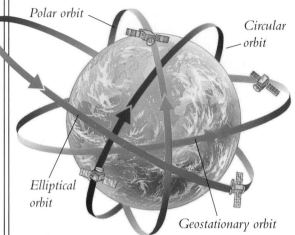

Polar orbit

Circular orbit

Elliptical orbit

Geostationary orbit

Types of orbits
Comsats and weather satellites are usually placed in geostationary orbits. This means that they always face the same part of the Earth. Polar orbits are often chosen for remote-sensing or scientific-survey satellites. As the satellite orbits from pole to pole, the Earth turns below it. In time, the satellite passes over every point on the Earth's surface.

A SATELLITE moves around the Earth in either a circular orbit or an elliptical orbit. It can be positioned in a polar orbit, circling the Earth from pole to pole, or placed in an equatorial orbit around the Equator. The satellite may cross the sky several times a day in a low Earth orbit (LEO), or hang in one place, in geostationary orbit. The type of orbit is chosen according to the satellite's function. Most communications and weather satellites are placed in geostationary orbit, 36,000km/22,300 miles above the Equator. A satellite in this orbit keeps pace with the turning Earth and appears to hang motionless over the same spot on the ground. Once a radio dish on the ground is aimed at it, the dish need not be moved again. Other satellites have to be tracked using movable radio dishes that follow the satellite as it crosses the sky. Try these two simple projects to see for yourself how geostationary orbits work and how satellites relay signals from one place to another.

GEOSTATIONARY ORBIT

You will need:
blue cardboard, red cardboard,
scissors, rope, a friend.

1 Cut out 14 strips of blue card and 30 strips of red card. Use the strips to mark a blue circle with a larger red circle around it on the ground. Hold one end of the rope and ask a friend to hold the other end.

2 Walk around the inner circle, while your friend walks around the outer circle. The blue inner circle represents the Earth, and the outer circle represents the orbit of a satellite around the Earth. If your orbiting friend keeps pace with you as you walk, your human satellite is in a geostationary orbit.

MAKE A SATELLITE RELAY

1 Using the scissors, cut out a rectangle of blue paper just big enough to cover the food can. Tape it in place. The food can will act as a ground-based radio receiver.

2 Measure out a 10cm x 10cm/4in x 4in piece of cardboard with the ruler. Cut it out and stick it to one side of the can. This will act as an antenna on your food-can receiver.

3 Place the food can on the floor. Take the ruler and lay it on the floor directly in front of the food can. Place it on the opposite side to the antenna, as shown.

You will need:
blue paper, scissors, food can, sticky tape, 1m ruler (yard stick), thin cardboard, flat mirror, modelling clay, torch (flashlight).

Satellite relays radio signals

Transmitter

Radio signals

Receiver

Redirecting radio waves
Comsats in geostationary orbit above the Equator enable radio transmissions to be sent to anywhere on the Earth's surface. Radio signals are transmitted from one side of the planet and aimed at the orbiting satellite. The comsat then relays (redirects) the signal to a receiver on the opposite side of the Earth.

4 Place the mirror on the ruler about 75cm/30in from the food can. The mirror will act like a satellite in geostationary orbit relaying signals. Fix it in place with modelling clay.

5 Darken the room. Place the torch beside the can, as shown. The torch will send out light beams in the same way that a ground-based transmitter sends out radio waves.

6 Switch on the torch. Move the mirror along the ruler. Keep moving it until the light beams are reflected off the mirror satellite and on to the antenna of the food can.

SPACEPLANES

Spaceplanes are vehicles that fly like aircraft while they are in the Earth's atmosphere and like spacecraft when they travel into space. The US Space Shuttle was a spaceplane. When it retired in 2011 after 135 space missions, astronauts travelled to and from the International Space Station in Russian Soyuz space capsules. Private companies, not government space agencies, are now developing a new generation of space planes. One of them, called *SpaceShipTwo*, is being developed to take paying passengers on short sub-orbital flights into space. *SpaceShipTwo* is based on an earlier spaceplane, *SpaceShipOne*, which made the first manned spaceflight by a privately-funded vehicle in 2004. Another spaceplane, *Dream Chaser*, is being developed to take cargo and astronauts to the International Space Station. Meanwhile, Boeing is developing a spaceplane called X-37, an experimental craft that will be used to test systems, materials and technologies for future space vehicles.

SpaceShipOne

This is a rocket-powered spaceplane designed to make sub-orbital spaceflights. In 2004, it won the US$10 million Ansari X Prize by making two manned spaceflights within two weeks. When it reaches its maximum altitude of over 100km/ 62 miles, it prepares to re-enter the atmosphere by raising the tail booms at the ends of its wings. This creates drag to slow the vehicle down as it falls back to Earth. It then glides to a landing on a normal airport runway.

SpaceShipTwo

SpaceShipTwo is being developed to carry a crew of two plus six passengers on sub-orbital spaceflights. It has been undergoing test-flights since 2010. Based on the design of SpaceShipOne, SpaceShipTwo is a bigger vehicle. It will soar into space at more than three times the speed of sound. As it falls back to Earth, the passengers experience six minutes of weightlessness. In addition to space tourists, it will also carry scientific instruments for space research. A fleet of SpaceShipTwo spaceplanes will operate from Spaceport America in New Mexico.

WhiteKnightTwo

SpaceShipTwo doesn't take off from the ground under its own power. Instead, it is launched in mid-air by a strange-looking mothership called WhiteKnightTwo, the biggest all-composite aircraft ever built. Powered by four jet engines, WhiteKnightTwo takes off with SpaceShipTwo tucked under the middle of its wing. When it reaches an altitude of 15,000m/49,200ft, SpaceShipTwo is released, fires its rocket and soars into space.

Dream Chaser

This is a mini Space Shuttle. It takes off sitting on the nose of an Atlas V rocket. At the end of its mission, perhaps carrying astronauts to the International Space Station, it re-enters the Earth's atmosphere at 25 times the speed of sound and glides down to a land on a runway. Dream Chaser has been making unmanned test-flights since 2012 and is expected to make its first crewed flight in around 2017.

Testing by computer

Computers are used to test the shape and performance of new aircraft and spacecraft. This avoids the expensive necessity of building scale models and prototypes at every stage. The computer simulation shown here uses false colours to show the stresses of a new design for a spaceplane.

Skylon

This is a model of a future orbital spaceplane called Skylon. It takes off from, and lands on, a runway like an airliner. The unique Sabre engines on its wing-tips operate as jet engines inside the atmosphere and as rocket engines in space. Skylon will be able to carry 15 tons of cargo into space or, by installing a pressurized module in its cargo bay, it could carry astronauts.

FACT BOX

• The first study of spaceplanes was made by German scientist Eugene Sänger in the 1930s.

• The first spaceplane was the North American X-15. Between 1959 and 1968, it made 199 flights, reaching a maximum altitude of 108km/67 miles and a top speed of 7,273kph/4,519mph.

• SpaceShipTwo is powered by a specially designed rocket motor, called RocketMotorTwo, which burns rubber with laughing gas (nitrous oxide).

Boeing X-37

Boeing's X-37 experimental spaceplane is launched inside a rocket nose cone. It will be capable of carrying out space missions including re-fuelling satellites and replacing faulty parts by using a robot arm.

The US Air Force is developing its own version of the X-37, called the X-37B Orbital Test Vehicle. It made its first orbital test-flight in 2010. Boeing plans to build yet another version, the X-37C, which will be able to carry six astronauts.

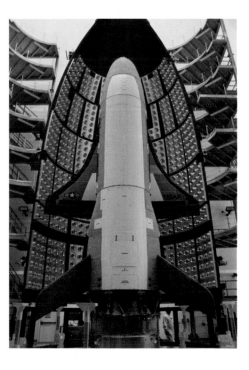

FUTURE PROJECTS

PREDICTING the future of space exploration is very difficult. It is likely that astronauts will walk on the Moon again, and that it will be possible to take holidays in space. It is far less likely that we will travel to the nearest stars in the forseeable future. No one knows exactly when, or if, these events will occur. Exploratory missions are planned to retrieve material from asteroids and to land on comets. This may eventually lead to asteroids being mined. Unmanned probes sent to survey Mars will send back further information to Earth about the planet, which could lead to the human exploration of Mars. Astronauts may return to the Moon in the near future to extract valuable minerals from its rocks and bring them back to Earth. Further in the future, a moonbase might serve as a staging post for human exploration of other planets in the Solar System.

Space station

Elevators

Space elevators
Space projects that seem impossible now may become reality in the very distant future. One day it may be possible to build a giant space station in geostationary orbit all the way around a planet. It could then be connected to the surface of the planet by spoke-like elevators.

Orion spacecraft
The Orion Multi-Purpose Crew Vehicle (MPCV) is a manned spacecraft being developed to carry four or more astronauts to the Moon or Mars. It might also carry cargo and astronauts to the International Space Station. Plans call for Orion to make an unmanned flight around the Moon and back to Earth in 2017 and its first manned flight some time after 2020.

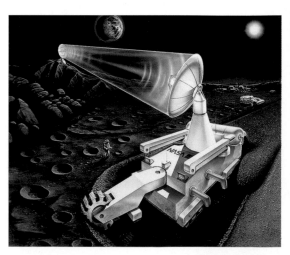

Living on the Moon
A moonbase could be built from pre-designed parts, such as the space station modules shown here. The first crews might spend six-month periods on the Moon. They would then build larger structures where people would eventually live for years at a time.

Moon mining
The Moon is rich in valuable materials that may one day be extracted by mining. In this artist's visualization, a solar-powered mining machine extract materials from the Moon's surface. Lunar soil contains large amounts of oxygen, silicon, iron, titanium and aluminium.

Mission to Mars

Orbital assembly

If the human exploration of Mars becomes a reality, it could begin with parts of a large interplanetary spacecraft being launched into Earth orbit. A future *Mars Explorer* vehicle might be launched in pieces by new ultra-powerful rockets developed from Space Shuttle components. It would then be assembled and tested in Earth orbit before leaving for Mars.

To the Red Planet

Mars Explorer 1's journey would take between four and nine months, depending on the flight path chosen. With the main spacecraft safely in orbit around Mars, the Lander craft would separate to enter the atmosphere and land on the Martian surface.

Surface transport

Mars mission astronauts might use roving vehicles to explore the Martian surface. Vehicles such as these would enable the astronauts to cover more ground on land surveys and on missions to pick up rock samples.

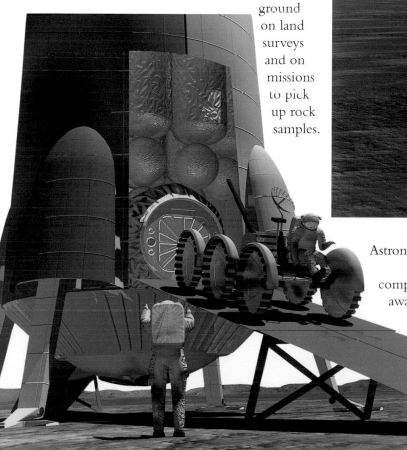

Shelter and fuel

Astronauts might live on Mars in a shelter sent on ahead of the mission. This artist's visualization (*above*) shows a completed Mars outpost in the background, about a mile away from the Lander craft. Fuel for the return journey to Earth might also be sent ahead, or else the astronauts could make it themselves on Mars. In the foreground, a propellant production facility has been set up next to the Lander. Methane and oxygen could be extracted from the atmosphere and used to fuel *Mars Explorer 1* for the return journey.

Index